LIVING THE CATHOLIC FAITH TODAY

Living the Catholic Faith Today

by

Most Reverend John F. Whealon, S.T.L., S.S.L., D.D
Archbishop of Hartford, Connecticut

Third Edition Revised

ST. PAUL EDITIONS

Photo credits:
  A. Alvarez—13
  DSP—cover, 18, 25, 36, 54, 61, 68, 85, 93, 97, 121
  Love Studio—31
  Dick Norton—101, 111

Library of Congress Cataloging in Publication Data

Whealon, John F.
    Living the Catholic faith today.

    1. Christian life—Catholic authors. I. Title.
BX2350.2.W48 1975   248'.48'2   75-6801

ISBN 0-8198-0491-6c
     0-8198-0492-4p

Printed in the U.S.A., by the Daughters of St. Paul
50 St. Paul's Ave., Boston, MA 02130

The Daughters of St. Paul are an international congregation of women
religious serving the Church with the communications media.

CONTENTS

Your Own Life

To work out a philosophy of life, it is necessary to begin with your own self. You need to see yourself as worthwhile, important, actually loved by God. You must begin with an honest, true view of your own self.

Your attitude towards yourself

The view that you have of your own self is, of course, of fundamental importance. Here is where many fail to learn the lessons taught by Christ. As a result, they get into many difficulties in living.

One of life's greatest challenges is to have the right attitude towards yourself. This is a devilishly complicated matter. Thomas Merton said of it all: "When we analyze it, it turns into a complex tangle of paradoxes. We become ourselves by dying to ourselves. We gain only what we give up, and if we give up everything we gain everything. We cannot find ourselves within ourselves, but only in others, yet at the same time, before we can go out to others we must first find ourselves. We must forget ourselves in order to become truly conscious of who we are…. But if we love ourselves in the wrong way, we become incapable of loving anybody else" ("No Man Is an Island," p. 16).

The basic, important attitude towards yourself might be pictured as having three qualities: (1) self-esteem; (2) self-forgetfulness; (3) self-balance.

Value

You need to have a clear idea of your own value and potential in life. Experts tell us today that many people—especially young people—have such a low opinion of their own worth that they despise, even hate themselves. And so, in a mood of self-hatred, they despair and treat themselves and others in a spirit of revenge.

But for the person who has accepted Jesus Christ and His teachings, life and self have an eternal value. Each one of us can say: "Christ shed His precious Blood for me. An 'amazing grace' has saved a sinner like me." Each one of us should think often of the loving kindness of the God who created us, of the generosity of God's Son who suffered to redeem us, of the fact that the Holy Spirit makes our body His temple of grace. We ought to think about the magnificent design of God that is shown in this body and in this creation around us.

Each one of us should see this life as of eternal importance because it is the introduction to an eternal life with God. We who have the faith know that our challenge is to take this life and make it as much like the Christ-life as possible. This is the Christ-life which St. Ignatius of Antioch called "our inseparable life." As the years go on, you are to mature to the fullness of Christ.

Self-forgetfulness

A second quality in your attitude towards self must be forgetfulness of self. This is the basic virtue of humility. You will get nowhere in the spiritual life if you live only within yourself and for yourself. You must in life come to a point where self is left behind, when you start living really for God and for others. This self-forgetfulness calls for a realization that self can be one's worst enemy and for a healthy amount of discipline.

"One of life's
greatest challenges
is to have the right
attitude towards
yourself."

The opposite of self-forgetfulness or humility is pride. Pride is the first of the capital sins, the cause of so much unhappiness in life, of so many grievances and criticisms, worries and broken marriages. Pride is self-love, and exists in the person who has not matured sufficiently to reach the humility which Christ demonstrated.

Balance

The third quality which you need in life is balance — keeping emotions and moods under control, not letting oneself go up and down emotionally like the ends of a see-saw, but staying in the middle.

Many years ago I read several "rules for living" set down by a Catholic, Dr. Raphael McCarthy. They have been helpful in giving pastoral advice to people who need to find or regain their balance. As Doctor McCarthy explained, these are largely taken from the Sermon on the Mount. In somewhat revised form, I give them to you as recommendations towards leading a balanced life.

1. Make your own happiness

So many people think they would be happy if only life's circumstances were changed: if they had a different job, if they had never married or had married someone else, if they had gotten married, if they had had different parents or education, if they were in a different religious community or seminary, if they lived elsewhere, had more money — or more possessions, etc. But the secret of happiness, like the kingdom of God, is within you. Take life the way God has given it to you, put a frame around it, and within that frame make your own happiness.

2. Live life one day at a time

God in His wisdom has given us life divided into days and nights. It is a wise man who learns to take each day as it comes, to put into that day its quota of prayer, work and education, and then to get a good, earned night's sleep in preparation for the next day. "Sufficient for the day is the evil thereof," said the Lord. We should not today think of yesterday's mistakes or of tomorrow's expectations of good or evil. Live in the living present, "heart within and God o'erhead."

3. Steer clear of worrying

Worry is a habit of mind that can be overcome. Youth and adolescence for so many people are a time of constant worry concerning what other people think of them. Maturity should end this, with the realization that God's estimate is what counts. Being true to one's finer self and Christlike ideals is the real norm. People who worry know that most of their worries never come to pass, and many others are not worth a worry. The daily viewpoint from eternity, that is, prayer, helps us keep our little concerns in perspective.

4. Work and keep yourself busy

Too many people have too little to do and so get into trouble. Have a list of projects that you plan to carry out in life. The education you give yourself is better than any received in school. Our society, our parishes and schools are desperate for helping hands and sympathetic hearts. Don't be disorganized; don't drift through life; don't let your intellect and soul gather cobwebs. Work creatively and keep yourself busy.

5. Make haste slowly

If you work, you deserve your rest and relaxation. Know how to relax; do not be tense, unable to sit still, unable even to read a book. The biblical day began in the evening—a reminder to get to bed in time to get a full night's rest. Be able to pace yourself. Do not think that you have to be constantly on the go. Make haste, but deliberately and slowly.

6. Cultivate decisive thinking

Too many people in life are really too disorganized to get a job done. You should be able to make decisions and to carry them out. One way to start accomplishing things is to be dissatisfied with bumbling, slipshod work, with letters unanswered and jobs unfinished. Make a list of things to do and do them. Have a list of projects to accomplish in life and accomplish them. You could go through life watching TV; but what would you accomplish for God, for others or for yourself? Cultivate decisive thinking.

7. Keep your sense of humor

A sense of humor is a "saving gift"; it will keep you from taking yourself too seriously and will help others along the road of life. Be able to laugh at yourself. As long as you are leading your religious life as well as possible, you should be able to relax, to avoid taking other and lesser things too seriously. This perhaps is why religious sisters, brothers and priests are so often people with an outstanding sense of humor.

8. Avoid self-pity

It is so easy to think and talk only of our own troubles, but that is like going through life looking at the end of our nose. It is but honesty to realize that most people in this world have far greater problems than we, and that most people have reason to envy us. All humans have crosses to carry. Life is a procession of people carrying crosses. When one carries his awkwardly, he causes trouble for others in line. The sane course to pursue is to play one's part in life cheerfully, courageously, with high trust in God — and without complaining or advertising one's troubles.

9. Want no thing in this world

So many people in life strive for one luxury after another, as if they could buy happiness. If and when you can say to yourself that there is really no material thing that you want or need, then you are close to wisdom and happiness. The unhappy king was told that he would find happiness by wearing the shirt of the poorest man in his kingdom, and discovered that the poorest man was cheerful and had no shirt at all.

10. Learn the value of silence

The omnipresent noises of radio and TV can certainly make life diverting, but they will keep you from thinking your own thoughts, from praying, from possessing your own soul in peace. You need some "quiet time" every day to develop your character, to educate yourself, to find God. Do not let modern electronics rob you of your own thoughts and prayers.

"There's nothing to be proud of any more" was the recent lament of one American to another. But there is. In this sense you ought to be humbly proud of your own eternal value, of the fact that Christ lived and died for you, and of the quality life which you are trying to life. With a proper, balanced view of your own worth, life starts to make sense. And life will make sense — because God loves you and has told you how to live.

"The real follower of Christ sees
Christ in every person he meets."

Your Attitude Towards Others

It is not easy to write about a person's attitudes towards other people. But it is important that we discuss these attitudes. Some people fall far short of the human and Christian ideal because they have never learned in life to think about others in the right way. They fail by being negatively critical, in thought first and then in word. Unknowingly, they spoil their chances of becoming like Christ.

No sweeping judgments about others

The Lord Jesus tells us how important it is not to pass negative judgments on others. This instruction of Christ is given in the Sermon on the Mount. The words and ideas are blunt: "If you want to avoid judgment, stop passing judgment. Your verdict on others will be the verdict passed on you. The measure with which you measure will be used to measure you. Why look at the speck in your brother's eye when you miss the plank in your own?" (Matthew 7:1-4)

It is, then, most important to avoid a negative and critical spirit. In our society today, as you so well know, criticisms abound. The way to make news today is to criticize someone. This is not in the sense of healthy, positive criticism, but in the sense of negative, destructive criticism against political figures, against religious leaders, against everyone.

The immature mind tends to make sweeping judgments and broad condemnations. The immature mind tends to describe things and people as "silly," "foolish," "ridiculous," etc. But our Lord forbade us to call one another "fools" (Matthew 5:22). For the immature mind, one side of a question is totally right, and the opposite side is totally wrong. Questions are seen as either black or white, with no intervening shades of gray.

Mature mind

The mature mind tends to avoid judgments and generalizations concerning others. The mature mind knows that so many questions are right or wrong not in a 90-10 proportion, but in a 51-49 balance. Most human activities, like the coded pictures sent back from our early Moon Rover, are made up of hundreds of different shades of gray.

The mature mind knows that, whenever human beings are involved, there is another side to the story. That side, like the far side of the moon, is rarely seen.

So the mature mind tends to reach conclusions and to express judgments with care, in exact language, with humility and exquisite sensitivity for the feelings of others. And in this, as in many things, we all fail often.

We notice, for example, these wise and humble words of Cardinal Gasquet at the end of his life: "Looking back on the years that have slipped away, it is on the basis of my personal experience that I confirm that certain decisions which I made under obedience, and which were quite contrary to what I considered right, proved to be the most just and the best. Even those which I looked upon as mistakes have given me, under obedience, results which in the end I had to acknowledge as truly providential."

In humility and honesty, then, we must avoid sweeping negative judgments. We must judge cautiously, exactly and charitably.

Always attribute good motives to others

The person living according to Christ must judge other people as charitably as possible. This means thinking of them, no matter what they have done, as innocent until proven guilty. So many go through this world thinking the opposite, judging people guilty until proven innocent. But the way of Christ and of common sense is to assign to others the highest motives.

There undoubtedly are scoundrels in our society. But most people are trying to do an honest job of living. If somehow we could get into the minds and souls of others, we would learn that they are basically decent and just people. When they do something wrong it is often because of ignorance, fear, loneliness. They may well be timid or unsure of themselves when they do it. They are not to be condemned. We should not throw stones at anyone else.

Positive and charitable

It is most important for us to view others in a positive and charitable way. The person with jaundiced eyes sees everyone and everything as yellow. The person whose windows are unwashed thinks the world is a dirty place. The Lord said: "You hypocrite! Remove the plank from your own eye first; then you will see clearly to take the speck from your brother's eye" (Matthew 7:5).

Be sincere in helping others

Once we have learned to forget self and to view others in positive fashion, then it becomes possible for us to know and to help other people. And if, in selfless fashion, we can help others along life's journey, then life is Christian. This is the virtue of love or charity that is our religion, as St. John tells us. This virtue of love is almost totally misunderstood by those who sing and write of it so much, as their lives sadly indicate. The virtue of love is a humble self-forgetfulness that precedes a total dedication to God and to others. In this way, as Christ demonstrated, God loves us. In this way we are to love God and all others who travel with us through life.

Lovingly

Much of this advice about one's attitude towards others is found in St. Paul's epistles—especially his letter to the Ephesians. Paul wrote: "I plead with you...to live a life worthy of the calling you have received, with perfect humility, meekness and patience, bearing with one another lovingly" (4:1-2). And also, "Get rid of all bitterness, all passion and anger, harsh words, slander, and malice of every kind. In place of these, be kind to one another, compassionate, and mutually forgiving, just as God has forgiven you in Christ" (4:31-32).

Paul's famous description of the virtue of Christian love tells each of us what we as other Christs should be. Using the adjectives and ideas of St. Paul (1 Corinthians 13:4-6), you can say to yourself: "I am to be patient. I am to be kind. I am not to be jealous. I am not to put on airs, nor to be snobbish. I am never to be rude. I am not to be self-seeking. I am not to be prone to anger, nor to brood over injuries. I am not to rejoice in what is wrong, but to rejoice with the truth."

Internal spirit

In a sense, the astonishing thing is that there are any Christians at all. If one takes it seriously, this is a most difficult religion to practice. It is small wonder that most people don't even try. This is a difficult religion not because of the few external rules and practices—but because of the internal spirit.

The real follower of Christ sees Christ in every person he meets. The true Christian is not proud or selfish or critical, does not start or continue quarrels, has no enemies, is careful not to judge others, is temperate in language.

In the midst of life today—with ridiculously inflated pride, greed, apathy, quarreling, sensuality—how healthy it is to know a real Christian, a genuine Catholic. As in the days of decadent Rome, may this people increase in number. May their spirit and example be contagious.

Your Attitude Towards Culture

The Man from Nazareth taught with clever little stories. These clever stories, or parables, delivered a deep spiritual lesson.

Matthew, Mark and Luke describe for us Christ's parables. All three give samples of parables, and give first the "Parable of the Sower." This was the little story of a farmer who, in Palestinian style, took handfuls of seed and, walking along, tossed the seed on the ground. The seed, broadcast, fell on shallow soil, on stony soil, among thorns, into good, deep, rich earth. The crop failed or grew up accordingly. Christ then identified the seed as God's message, and the various soils as souls of people who are shallow, worldly, greedy, sincere, etc.

It is a parable not of the farmer-sower, nor of the seed, but really of the type of soil. The hope of the harvest is in the topsoil. Topsoil builds up, we are told, at the rate of about a foot every century. It is made up of the accumulated dust, rotted vegetable matter, leaves, the worn out products of nature, of nature's storms and rains of untold yesteryears.

The seed is God's Word, the message of Jesus Christ. It has fallen into your soul, your life. What kind of topsoil have you supplied for it? Hopefully a good, deep soil, developed by your own thinking and praying, silences, your mistakes and crosses of the past. Hopefully you are not a shallow individual, or a person in whom this message has taken root, "but anxieties over life's demands, and the desire for wealth, and cravings of other sorts come to choke it off" (Mark 4:19).

It is important, then, to supply good soil for the message of Christ. This is pre-evangelization. I now write about three of those necessary attitudes which you must have to receive God's Word. They are a right attitude towards money, towards education and towards culture. If your values are sorted out concerning these, you will be better able to accept Christ and follow the Christian and Catholic way of life.

Money

The attitude of a person towards money is, in the teachings of Jesus Christ, of crucial importance. The Master warned us that money is a greater danger than anything else for His followers. These storm warnings are clear in the Gospels—"You cannot serve God and mammon..." "How hard it is for a rich man to enter the kingdom of heaven..." "Do not lay up for yourselves treasures on earth..." "Blessed are the poor in spirit."

The problem, as the Lord warns, is attachment to money and to the things of this earth. It is a part of fallen human nature to want more and more, to get absorbed in what money can buy, to make the things and pleasures of this passing earth the end-all and the be-all here. And then the spiritual values fade away—especially any idea of taking up the cross each day, of working out one's salvation in fear and trembling. Then people forget that this short life and its possessions decay and turn into dust. That their earthly needs are only irritating grains of sand compared to their needs for eternity.

The problem is attachment to money. We must be careful of generalizing. Among the affluent are some deeply religious people and among the poor are some unspiritual and materialistic people—and vice versa. But there is far greater danger to one's eternal salvation in affluence than in poverty.

Generally speaking, Christians have not done spiritually a good job with affluence. Though the principles are in the New Testament, we Christians have not learned how to handle wealth. Too many have lost their sense of values when they

"The first day of every week is given to us as a 'little Easter.' It is a day for worship—and also for religious and cultural renewal."

became materially rich. True wealth, in fact, is not a matter of annual income. All those who read these words are more wealthy in daily living than King Herod or Queen Cleopatra ever dreamed of being.

It is unfortunate that the Biblical idea of tithing has never received much acceptance from Catholic people. It has so much to recommend it, especially when we are all being asked constantly to donate to this or that good cause. The idea is simply to give ten percent of income to God: five percent to the parish; the other five percent to good causes and charities, civic as well as religious, and especially to the poor. Tithing brings peace of mind and God's blessings.

A Gospel ideal in life is simplicity. Do not clutter up your life with things and miss the essentials. As Thoreau wrote so well: "A man is rich in proportion to the number of things which he can afford to let alone," and "Our life is frittered away by detail.... Simplify, simplify."

This lesson is important.

Education

Your attitude towards educating yourself will make a difference in receiving the teaching of Jesus Christ. Sad to say, the prevailing attitude in our nation towards education has harmed the religious lives of many.

Education in America of modern times is among our greatest failures as a nation. We have an elaborate, expensive, available and obligatory program of education. Yet most Americans get an education primarily to make more money. Many with a high-school diploma or college degree do not continue to study or learn after leaving school. They do not read. They are no longer inquisitive. They talk only to repeat what was said on the radio or TV.

What is education? It is a lifelong process of learning. What you got in school was meant to be just a beginning. You should then be learning more every day. You should read. Try to discuss questions in depth. You should, if you can, attend some of the special classes and night courses that are so available. And you should beware of getting dependent on TV or radio so that you give up serious reading or study.

The alert Catholic has so much to study. You can learn Scripture from the "New American Bible." You can get a course in Church history from Daniel-Rops' "History of the Catholic Church." You can learn theology from the documents of Vatican II.

Keep your mind alert, flexible, exercised—and you will be a more religious person.

Culture

Your attitude toward culture is also quite important. "Culture" means values which a person treasures, and which cannot be bought or measured with money.

The Catholic Church has been historically a mother of culture. Many magnificent national traditions, outstanding music and art, have developed in Catholic nations. An appreciation of such a cultural heritage was brought over to the New World by the poor immigrant ancestors of most of us. They were rich because of their cultural traditions and religious faith. They tried to hand on this culture and faith to their descendants.

What have you done with these cultural traditions? Have you preserved your national heritage, your family feasts and customs? Are you a person who has a taste for quality music and art? Do you have good religious art in your home? If you are surrounding your life with these quality products from your own Catholic and national heritage, then you will be helped towards a quality Catholic life.

The modern Catholic who has lost these values of Catholic culture will find living religiously more difficult. And the young Catholic growing up to the tune of beat music and a drive-in restaurant level of culture will find it more difficult to live the Christ-life in depth.

It is not difficult to develop here a cultural life. World-famous museums may be nearby. We can have even symphonic music on records and tapes and live in concert halls. There are famous Catholic shrines nearby, or even at a distance, that should be visited in pilgrimage.

The special day for developing culture is Sunday, the Lord's day. The first day of every week is given to us as a "little Easter." We are to look upon every Sunday as a day for worship—and also for religious and cultural renewal. We are to keep this day holy by participating in Mass. We are also to avoid all activities that would hinder renewal of soul and body—such as needless work and business activities, unnecessary shopping, etc. The purpose of all this is to make Sunday a day of personal renewal each week, a day of genuine culture. Your approach to Sunday, then, is a sign and a test of your level of Catholic culture.

Your Attitude Towards Sex

Sex and marriage are much talked about and much written about these days. But rarely does a person hear about the need for a healthy and balanced attitude towards sex so as to lead a life in Christ.

Many Americans are losing their spiritual sense because of false attitudes towards sex. Many Catholics today are weakened in their faith because of this. And many become incapable of accepting Christ and the Christian way simply because of their views on sex.

It has been called "the Sexual Revolution." As a result, Americans today are overwhelmed with rather open and crass sexuality from advertisements, newspapers, television, books, films, magazine displays, and the manner of dress of many people. In the midst of all this, how does the follower of Christ go about the work of salvation? In an "everybody-is-doing-it" atmosphere, how should a religious-minded person react?

This is a serious problem. It is much more of a problem for the young — who are always strongly tempted to follow the crowd and not to be different.

The contemporary follower of Christ should know that this problem is an old one. When the Apostle Paul started preaching Christ to the Mediterranean world, he ran directly into the pervasive existence of sexual temptations on all sides of converts to Christ. Corinth, for example, was a port city notorious for moral depravity. It had pagan religions that even made prostitution a part of their religious practice. Ephesus, as another example, had an infamous temple to the goddess Diana or Artemis, a goddess of fertility.

So the instructions given by Paul to those early Christians are of considerable help to us who face the same problems today. You would be helped by studying Paul's instructions about the Christian attitude towards sex. Helpful study references are Romans 12:1-2, First Corinthians 6:15-20, Galatians 5:13-26, Ephesians 4:17-24 and 5:3-7, Philippians 2:15-16, Colossians 3:1-10, First Thessalonians 4:1-8, and the description of a godless sexual society in Romans 1:24-32.

For your life, nothing much need be added to these instructions from Paul to the Ephesians: "As for lewd conduct or promiscuousness or lust of any sort, let them not even be mentioned among you; your holiness forbids this. Nor should there be any obscene, silly, or suggestive talk; all that is out of place. Instead, give thanks. Make no mistake about this: no fornicator, no unclean or lustful person — in effect an idolator — has any inheritance in the kingdom of Christ and of God. Let no one deceive you with worthless arguments. These are sins that bring God's wrath down on the disobedient; therefore have nothing to do with them" (5:3-7).

The temptations in modern society, like a whirlpool, carry along and carry down into the vortex those people who get too close to them. The spirit of this world takes over at an early age, when youngsters are in elementary school. Some youngsters become absorbed in the body, pad and dress themselves in pagan, exhibitionistic fashion. They fall into a pattern of early exclusive dating that weakens rather than develops character. They marry when young and unprepared; they accept contraception. When their own consequent character weaknesses show through, the marriage is in deep trouble. It is no wonder that our society is so con-

"Marriage is for the strong of character who are prepared to carry out the awesome responsibility of life according to God's laws in mutual love and carrying on the human race."

cerned about venereal disease, sex education in schools, the shocking rate of divorce. We wonder about the effects of so much weak selfishness on the next generation. This is actually discrimination against their own children.

One hears these days of some attempts to justify pre-marital sex, contraception, marriage after divorce. Even in Catholic circles such views are occasionally heard. But attempts to justify such actions are usually based on a life-view that rules out any idea of sin. This view holds that only a Puritan or a neurotic worries about sin, about what is right and wrong. So—just live naturally: everything that is human is good. "Love" is good. Besides, everyone else is living this way.

But Jesus Christ, the Ten Commandments, the teachings of St. Paul and the Church all testify to the true Christian attitude towards sex and marriage. A person cannot follow Christ and at the same time joke with the devil. You cannot serve God and Venus. Sex is one department of God's plan for life—but other departments of life are more important. Sex is sacred, to be safeguarded by modesty and avoidance of any occasion of sin. Marriage is for the strong of charac-ter who are prepared to carry out the awesome responsibility of life according to God's laws in mutual love and carrying on the human race.

Contraception

The "dark night of the soul" that is the problem of con-traception has not yet ended for the Church. Medical sci-ence is developing an increasingly satisfactory approach to family planning that squares with the moral law. The temptations towards contraception are powerful and under-standable. Not enough have the knowledge and discipline to use the approved natural family planning programs—and this is a major pastoral challenge for the Church. In the spir-it of "Humanae Vitae" we must be sympathetic towards those who fail—but must never compromise God's plan for marriage. A morally acceptable method of family planning is available to married couples to observe God's law. We should thank medical science for its help in this human problem. But we should especially pray that married people will have the faith, generosity and wisdom to recognize children as "the supreme gift of marriage."

Modesty

The very word "modesty" is rarely heard. It is a virtue. A virtue is a strong or manly quality in a person. Modesty does not refer only to sexual matters, and means not exhibiting or showing off oneself. In sexuality, modesty means that one dresses, talks and acts in such a way as never to cause temptation for another.

To dress modestly is a challenge for women in this openly immodest age. Yet this is not an impossible challenge, as many women of religious convictions and common sense are demonstrating.

Monsignor Knox once wrote that virginity in the world should not be a negative idea — but it should be something positive and magnificent, like a parade coming down the street. So, in this exhibitionistic and suggestive age, should be the modesty of a sincere follower of Christ.

The modest and Christian person will on principle have absolutely nothing to do with pornographic literature, X-rated movies, pagan stage plays, filthy jokes, etc. The "Playboy philosophy" is erotic idolatry of the human body. The Christian philosophy accepts the body as God's sacred creation, not to be commercialized; accepts marriage as God's plan for a lifelong union till death; and sees fornication and adultery as horrendous evils.

Early marriages

The mistake being made by so many is to get married too early in life. Marriage calls for proven maturity of character. Our American society and our Catholic society would be better—and countless people would be benefited—if the average age for marriage were at least ten years later than at present. One should be well established—in life, in character, in religion—before assuming the responsibilities of marriage.

The divorced Catholic

The dilemma of the divorced Catholic is a pastoral challenge for the Church. Many Catholic marriages have failed. The Lord's teachings on marriage are a "hard saying"—that what God has joined together no man is to put asunder, and that one who marries a divorced person commits adultery.

The divorced Catholic needs special guidance—guidance not to become bitter, not to talk about "rules of the Church" when these are the rules of Christ, guidance to overcome feelings of loneliness and desolation in keeping with the eternal teachings of Christ, to keep close to the sacraments, especially Holy Communion. And encouragement never to enter into an invalid marriage, because that cuts one off from receiving the life-giving and life-sustaining sacraments.

Sometimes divorced and remarried Catholics may have reason to suspect that their first marriage was not a true marriage before God, because of some serious defect in the contract or in one of the persons. Such a situation should be discussed with a canon lawyer or knowledgeable priest or deacon to see if there is any chance for a declaration of nullity on the previous marriage.

For those living in an invalid marriage, the religious problems are greater and the need for compassion and counseling is also greater. Such Catholics must never lose hope or lose sight of salvation. They should by all means remain faithful to Sunday Mass, parish life and personal prayer. It is a difficult way to live and reach salvation—but the mercy of God is great, especially to the contrite of heart.

The breakdown of sexual discipline in a life has serious effects. When sex is used in a worthy manner it can encourage one to great virtue, love and even heroic sacrifice. But when sex is abused, especially through stubborn habits, its qualities are reversed.

Repeated sins of impurity can lead to distaste for prayer and spiritual values. Repeated sins of impurity can darken understanding, inflate egoism and pride, decrease genuine love, weaken religious faith. It is easy to see the effect of impurity on a person's spiritual life, on the spirit of worship and liturgical participation, on social concern, on helping other people. The breakdown of sexual morality can weaken the moral fiber of society and drain the mental energy of people.

There is need, in the present age, for each of us to rein-force our convictions about the standards of sexual morality expected of every follower of Jesus Christ. All are sinners, as the Bible says — and there must be compassion on those who fail. But this clear and helpful part of the Christian message needs to be heard, understood and followed in the face of the adverse tide now threatening our society.

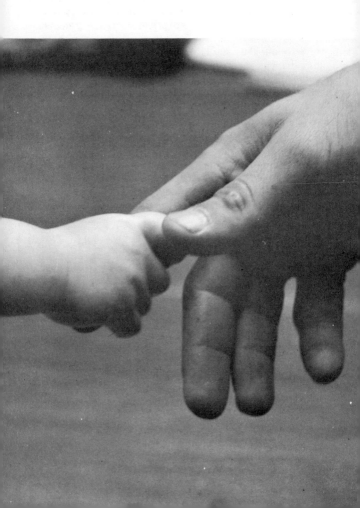

"Believe in God? Considering the incredible design of this human body, the believer is the logical person. It is the agnostic or the atheist who has problems."

Why Believe in God?

For any non-believer of clear intellect and mature personality, the first major religious challenge is whether God exists at all.

Is there a God? Is there a God above and beyond us all? Above our life and death, above our joys and sorrows, above our world and space program? For thinking people, this is really the important question. Is there a God?

People have been asking this question for as long as people have been thinking. But now so much more is known about this world and about ourselves. There are answers and ideas never known before. The great thinker, Thomas Aquinas, lived in the 13th century. Not until the 17th century did man discover the microscope, cell structure, the circulation of blood, etc. Much of what is known about the world has been learned in recent scientific studies.

For me, the strongest reasons for believing in God are shown by the human body. Modern medical science says much about the remarkable design of that body—a design which in many thousands of ways advertises the most careful, amazingly intelligent planning. In asking yourself whether there is a God, think about that design—far more clever than the design of any automobile, any watch, any piece of machinery. You own a body. Think—really think—about it.

Here are some reasons why your body is a product made by a most Intelligent Designer:

Your skull and brain

The human brain is the control center for the senses and nerves. It is the place for reasoning, memory, decision-making. The skull protecting this brain is made of tough, hard bone. Light but strong, it is shaped into a design that makes architects and engineers admire its strength. Scientists do not yet understand how a person remembers or thinks or feels. But they know the brain is an unbelievably complicated center of communications. The brain has 10 billion cells that never sleep, and these cells are linked with billions of inter-connectors. It is an electro-chemical network that runs the body. In some brain areas a hundred million cells fit into a cubic inch, and every one is connected to at least 60,000 others. It is an awesome mass, sophisticated, untiring, elaborately protected.

Your eyes

The way in which you see things—see this printed material—is because of incredible design. The back of the eye, or retina, is part of the brain itself. Your eye is a camera, with the size of the pupil adjusting to light and the eyeball adjusting to distance, so that light rays focus on your retina. The retina has 125 million tiny rods and several million cones, so that your brain gets the picture, and in technicolor. There are even chemical adjustments for night vision. The eye sees at one time several hundred million visual fragments, and the brain pieces them together and interprets them to see the important things.

Your eyelids

The eyeball is bathed, behind and in front, by a salt water that cleans it. The water is constantly being manufactured. The tear system is the admiration of any designer. There are glands to produce tears, two drainpipes to carry excess water down to the nose, grease glands to protect the lower lids, and even a special chemical in the water to destroy bacteria. And all this is fitted into such a compact space.

Your ears

Here the sound waves enter the ear, and bitter wax inside the ear keeps insects away from the ear canal. The eardrum vibrates, and three tiny bones in the middle ear magnify this wave motion 22 times. A tube is there to keep air pressure equal. The inner ear is a jewel of design, with an arrangement to soften the overly harsh sounds. The sound wave then travels to the great auditory nerve which has 25,000 fibres.

Whittaker Chambers regained his faith in God one day when watching his daughter at her breakfast. "My eye came to rest on the delicate convolutions of her ear—those intricate, perfect ears. The thought passed through my mind: '...they could have been created only by immense design.' The thought was involuntary and unwanted.... If I had completed it, I should have had to say: Design presupposes God."

Your balance

There is a device built into your skull to register tipping, and to enable you to correct tilting and to hold your balance. This also is a jewel-like design, with three parts, and is not yet well understood by medical scientists.

Your repair system for cuts

Cut yourself, and there follows an astonishing process. In the flowing blood is a programmed arrangement. The blood itself clots and glues, forming a firm fabric, and then under the clot the flat surface forms itself into flat surface cells. It is all a masterpiece of design—and quite a problem for the atheist.

Your program of rebuilding

Your entire body is being constantly rebuilt, so that after seven years it is entirely new. The body uses and reuses materials in frugal fashion. Each kidney is a magnificently designed purification machine, with over one million elements called nephrons.

Your saliva

The spit or saliva in your mouth is there in exactly the right amount and thickness, thanks to three pairs of salivary glands. It comes out as watery when you need to spit, and as thick when you need lubrication for chewing and swallowing. You develop around a quart of saliva each day. This keeps your mouth moist and clean and reduces friction around your tongue and teeth. Your saliva even has a special chemical enzyme that starts digesting food. The Russian Pavlov studied 50 years to learn these wonders of saliva.

Your skin

This skin is a remarkable protection against heat, cold, sun, water, danger, disease, and injury. It reports to the brain any pain, weight, heat, cold. The body heat comes from the intense activity of your liver, kidneys and heart. The skin radiates this heat. In cold weather the skin holds more of the heat. In warm weather it opens the pores and lets off more heat. When it is hot, the two million sweat glands produce sweat—and the surface evaporation becomes your personal air conditioning system. There are 10-15 thousand million nerve tracks which report to the brain. Tanning is a clever defense of the skin against harmful sun rays.

Your nose

When you breathe in air, it must be filtered. It passes through a network of hairs, and then through a series of narrow passages with sudden turns and with moist, warm walls. So the filtering hairy trap of the nostrils and the chang-ing directions of air flow through sticky nasal linings bring clean air to the lungs. Every time you blow your nose there is a reminder of the effectiveness of your air filtering system.

Your hand

Medical science has learned of the "hand brain" — the huge communications center in the brain that controls the hand and which shows the importance of the hand. The hand is a marvel of design, with the thumb able to put itself against each finger, with the fingers able to fold over and grasp an object, and with a protective, useful nail growing at the end of fingers and thumb.

Your spinal column

This "backbone" is a most successful compromise be-tween rigidity and flexibility. Thanks to it the person can stand upright and still can bend and turn, and at the same time it carries the main communications link of the body.

When you think, really think about the wonder that is your body — then you will wonder how this body could be, unless it had been designed by the most brilliant Architect and made by the most efficient Maker. This body has grown from a single cell to 1,000,000,000,000,000 cells, with each doing its job as designed. Every minute of human life is an achieve-ment greater, more amazing, than any flight to space, than any working of a large city or nation.

At times people say or think that "evolution" is respon-sible for the design of man's body. But evolution is no explana-tion unless it is planned by an intelligent designer. No matter how great the need, "evolution" could never develop a heart or hand, ear wax or fingernails, nostril hairs or saliva. Suppose that for millions of years there were ants getting into the skull through the ears, or people bleeding to death because cuts or wounds would not heal, or fingers without fingernails.

The only way these problems could be solved was for an Intelligence somewhere, somehow saying "This is a problem. This must be solved. This is how it will be solved." The design of the human body absolutely demands a planning intelligence. That intelligence of course could have used a gradual development of evolution if it so wished—an evolution with God behind it.

There are other ways for people to find God—the fact that this world is just at the right distance from the sun; the qualities of air, of water, of saltwater; green plants and chlorophyll; nuclear physics and the quantum ladder; the molecular structure of the human body; the instincts of animals; the instincts of us humans; the enormous variety and beauty of it all. We have everything for human life. Nothing is missing. In the Biblical sense, it all is good.

Believe in God? Considering the incredible design of this human body, the believer is the logical person. It is the agnostic or the atheist who has problems. He cannot understand, cannot explain, cannot move ahead any further to know what it is all about. For all this design to happen by chance is similar to a mindless ape striking at random the keys of a typewriter and accidentally typing the entire Encyclopedia Britannica.

The first words of the Creed are "I believe in God." In modern times you can and should say it, mean it and have no apologies for it. And if you believe in God, you can move on to further steps in building your house of religious faith on a solid foundation.

Why Make Jesus
Your Personal Lord?

Imagine that you are an astronaut, standing on the gray sterile moon. Against the blackness of space you see earth. It is about the size of a tennis ball held at arm's length. There it hangs — blue, green, white, brown — beautifully colored. Majestically turning. Just the right distance from the sun. It is an "oasis in space," well-watered, surrounded with a protective atmosphere. It is actually a huge spaceship in orbit around the sun. Then you think about the passengers on that ship. They come into existence, live there for a brief lifetime, and die. So you think about the old, old questions. Granted that there is a Designer — and that this is all the result of very careful design — but what is the purpose of it all? What is the master plan? Where do we come from? Is there something we are to do in our lifetimes? Are there rules for us to follow? After we die is there just nothing, or is there a life after death?

These old questions have special meaning in the space age. Now the world and human life are known as being even more extraordinary in this universe.

Where do we look for an answer to the meaning of it all? We can find many philosophies and religions to tell us how to live wisely with human wisdom. But there is only one which claims to tell us God's master plan for this world and for all men. That religion is Christianity, and the one who claimed to give us the story is Jesus Christ.

Who was Jesus Christ? The best way to learn about Him is to get a copy of the Gospels. These are four pamphlets, written in the first century A.D. As records, the Gospels are more solid than any other documents of that time. The Gospels tell quite a story. You will be able to think and talk about that story if you begin, for example, with the short Gospel of Mark.

It is a fascinating story, told in somewhat breathless fashion, by men who had just learned God's grand design for life. The story centers on the meaning and the teaching of Jesus Christ.

Jesus Christ — who was He? The Gospels tell of Jesus as a good Jewish man, an heir to religious beliefs and traditions going back to Moses and to Abraham. Among those beliefs was the expectation that God, who loved this chosen Jewish people, would some day send a special prophet — the Messiah.

Jesus lived in Palestine. He was a journeying teacher who, like others, gathered around Him certain disciples. He taught, using simple words and ideas, how to live. That a person should forget self...be totally dedicated to others...refuse to judge or criticize others...love God first and then all men...be prayerful...be pure in life and thought...live in simple, poor fashion. It was and is quite a way of life. You can get a good idea of it from the Sermon on the Mount (St. Matthew's Gospel, Chapters 5-7).

The life led by Jesus Christ was the perfect life. It does not take long to locate in the Gospels the teachings and examples of His personal qualities. He was humble. He was deliberately poor and uncomplicated. He was pure, and taught purity of mind as well as body. He was hard working and dedicated. He was tough and blunt. He was always patient. He was given to constant daily prayer. He told His followers to stay away from negative judgments about others. He told them to be childlike in their simplicity. He taught His followers to be unselfish, always forgiving, to be forgetful of self and concerned about all others, and to "carry the cross" every day of life.

"The life led by Jesus Christ
was the perfect life.... He was humble.
He was deliberately poor and
uncomplicated. He was pure...
hard working and dedicated."

All this He taught, and this is what He obliged His followers to do. This is real Christianity, this daily imitation
of the perfect life: "In a word, you must be made perfect as
your heavenly Father is perfect" (Matthew 5, 48) ..."Come to
me, all you who are weary and find life burdensome, and I will
refresh you...learn from me, for I am gentle and humble of
heart" (Matthew 11:28-29).

But there was more to this Jesus of Nazareth than the
perfect life. He worked remarkable miracles, as you will
notice from reading the Gospels. And He claimed that the
miracles proved God was with Him. Jesus was guaranteeing
by miracles the truth of His teaching—and the Fourth Gospel
makes this clear.

The greatest of the miracles was the Resurrection of
Christ from the dead—a miracle which His own Apostles first
refused to believe. As has well been said, the best way to start
a new religion is to have yourself crucified and buried, and
then to rise from the dead on the third day.

But there is something deeper to Jesus Christ—something even more mysterious. He claimed not only to be the
expected Messiah, but claimed also to be united with God
Himself. Jesus made references to existing even before His
birth in Palestine, and claimed to be divine—the "Son of
God" in a mysterious and true sense.

The Gospels state that God actually came to this world,
in the person of Jesus Christ, in order to tell all of us the
master plan. God became man. The technical name for this
is "Incarnation"; the day when Christians celebrate it is
Christmas. When God became man, this was the greatest
demonstration of God's concern and love for us human
beings. So we call Christ the "First One," or "First-Born,"
of all men. He somehow unites and stands at the head of all
men.

But there is a further idea which we must understand
about the life and works of Jesus. Not only did the God-man
teach and show us how to live and die, but He also, by His

life, death, resurrection and ascension actually made it possible for us to get forgiveness for sins and to become a child of God. This is the work of Christ as "Savior" and "Redeemer" of the world. Christ went to His cruel death on behalf of sinful man. By this, His most holy death, He redeemed the human race from the slavery of sin and of the devil, and made it possible for men to become the adopted sons of God and to live with God after our death. This is why we who believe in Jesus call Him our Savior and Redeemer. We remember our redemption especially on Good Friday and Easter Sunday. In fact every Sunday is a "little Easter."

There is in Jesus Christ a depth of mystery that is beyond us—the mystery of Jesus Christ, born of His mother who was a virgin, who lived a poor life, who suffered, died and rose for us. Jesus Christ—that mysterious, appealing, wonderful person. As William Langland wrote 600 years ago in his Vision of Piers Plowman: "Jesus Christ of heaven, in the apparel of a poor man, pursues us always." Jesus Christ is your Hound of Heaven who will pursue you through life, wherever you go, until you come to terms with Him.

Who was Jesus Christ? As the Gospels say, whose Son is He? Was He a wild dreamer who made fantastic claims—or was He just a good man set up on a pedestal by His followers—or was He the Son of God who came to this world to tell us God's master plan and show us how to live?

There is no real way in which we can view the Gospels as imaginative forgeries. They came from that time and place. They tell of men convinced against their will of the truth of Jesus Christ, of His miracles and teachings.

What were the basic teachings of Christ? They were that God the Creator is a loving Father who cares for His children, that the way for man to live is to follow the teachings and living example of the Son of God, that judgment and eternal life follow death in this world.

There is then a magnificent plan to it all—to all of life. It is not a "tale told by an idiot, signifying nothing." It is the result of God's love — a love to which we are expected to respond. We are to know God, to love Him and serve Him in this life so as to be happy with Him forever in heaven.

It is the resurrected Christ who proves and guarantees all this. For the Apostles the Resurrection was like an atomic blast which changed all living.

So this Catholic Christian faith must pay great attention to the person of Jesus Christ. You must study Him, know Him, love Him. You must imitate Him. You must, in these modern times, live in Christ. He must be your way of life.

You must accept completely Jesus Christ as God's Son and as your personal model in living. In Gospel words, you too must make Jesus your Lord.

Why Be a Roman Catholic?

An airline executive talked about his workers: "Our airline is the most successful in the world. But we're up to our neck in problems — religious problems. We can't do a good job unless a lot more of our stewardesses, pilots and sales-people are able to figure out what their lives are all about."

It makes good sense to say "I believe in God." It makes good sense to say "I believe in Jesus Christ." Where do you go from there?

Many people go nowhere from there. Yes, they accept God and they accept Christ — in one way or another. But they do not want to get involved in any church. Older people do not want to be "tied down." Younger people are not joiners. Look at the kind of people who go to church every Sunday, they like to say. And some of those priests and ministers are, they say, poor advertisements for any church.

These are all only excuses. They are not important. They are not the real question. The real question is whether the idea of "church" came from Jesus Christ. If it is His idea, His plan and will — then it is your job to join, whether you like it or not.

Here is where knowing the New Testament is helpful. Study the Gospels. See how Jesus Christ picked out 12 men whom He called apostles. Christ gave them special attention and training, and promised to make them the foundation of His Church. Christ gave them a leader or shepherd, told them to teach with authority in His name, and promised to be with them to the end of the world.

If you read the later New Testament books, you will see how that little Church faced many problems, but kept on growing. The Church was described as the "bride of Christ"...also as a Body, with Christ the head and ourselves the members. So the New Testament describes for us the Church — started by Christ Himself, built on the apostles, directed by the apostle Peter, and ordered to teach the "good news" until the end of the world.

Thus, if you accept Jesus Christ, you have to accept His Church. It is a package deal. As the New Testament shows, there is no way to follow Christ outside the Church. There is no churchless Christianity.

So the idea of a church makes good sense. We are supposed to help one another. We are not alone in this life, and we are not to be alone in following Christ and leading the Gospel way of life. The Church is really the "people of God." Following Christ is not a "do it yourself" project. It is something we do with others, helping others and being helped by others.

But which church should a person belong to? There are so many different Christian churches, and each one has its history, traditions, good people, etc. — as well as its weaknesses. Today there are many followers of Christ who are working and praying for Christian unity. Christ prayed at the Last Supper "that they all may be one." This splintering of Christianity is wrong. It is confusing for the person searching for truth.

Until Christian unity is found, where does a person go who wants to carry out the plan of Christ?

With respect for all Christian groups, the Roman Catholic Church has special qualities. The Catholic Church notes how

"Why...the Roman Catholic Church? Simply put—because in the light of the New Testament and history, this is the Church programmed and established by the Lord Jesus Christ."

Christ was careful to give special responsibilities to one of the apostles. The Master gave to the one named Simon the new name "Rock" (Peter), and stated that He would build His Church on that Rock. Christ told Peter to strengthen the faith of the other apostles. And after the Resurrection, the Lord actually appointed Peter as Shepherd of the entire flock (that is, the Church), and instructed him to feed and care for all in that flock.

The Catholic Church goes back in history to Christ and the Apostles. It has been in this world for nearly 2,000 years, teaching the Gospel and trying to make people holy and Christ-like. The makeup of the Catholic Church goes back to the original plan of Christ: its bishops have succeeded the apostles; and the one bishop who succeeded Peter (the Bishop of Rome) still is Shepherd for the entire Church.

What are the special qualities of the Roman Catholic Church? I point out three of them. First — its historical connection with the Apostles and with Christ. Second — its teaching authority, found in the Bishop of Rome (the Pope) with the other bishops, so that a Catholic can be certain of what to believe. Third — its seven Sacraments. These are special helps in life towards holiness.

It is a remarkable, warm, precious old institution, this Catholic Church. It has carried the burdens of 20 centuries of history. It has spread the Gospel of Christ across the world, in spite of great difficulties. It has produced many great saints and outstanding popes — and also some disappointments and failures. It is the oldest Christian church — and in a sense the youngest also, for it has just had an updating by the Second Vatican Council.

But a person should not join the Catholic Church because of likes or dislikes. In the same way, a Catholic does not stay in the Church or leave the Church because of the way things are being done — or are not being done. A person should be a Catholic by conviction. Of the greatest importance are the claims of this Church to be true — to have the fullness of truth. To back up its claims, the Catholic Church asks you to use your God-given intelligence, to study the New Testament, to go back in history, to work out the really important questions in your life.

With these ideas I have not given you the exact quotations or references from the New Testament. To give all of them would perhaps confuse the reader. But to find them, just take out your New Testament and read these chapters: in St. Matthew's Gospel, Chapters 16, 18 and 28; in St. Mark's Gospel, Chapter 16; in St. Luke's Gospel, Chapter 22; and in St. John's Gospel, Chapters 14 and 21. Then continue your reading: Acts of the Apostles, Chapters 1 and 5; the First Letter to the Corinthians, Chapter 12; the Letter to the Colossians, Chapter 1; and especially the Letter to the Ephesians, Chapters 1, 2, 4 and 5.

Why should you belong to the Roman Catholic Church? Simply put — because in the light of the New Testament and of history, this is the Church programmed and established by the Lord Jesus Christ.

"We show in life...how thankful we are by believing what God tells us is true...."

What Are the Main Teachings of Catholic Faith?

Suppose that you are working out a personal philosophy of life. You know that there is a God. You are ready to accept Jesus Christ as a messenger from God who brought the "Good News" about the real meaning of life and death. And, after comparing many religions and many Christian religions, you have found that the Catholic Church is the one which carries out the plan of Christ and the will of God for yourself.

The next step is an easy one. It is simply to learn what the Catholic Church teaches. You are ready to believe because you know that this Church has authority and is guaranteed to teach the truth.

Don't let yourself get confused about the teachings of the Church. The basic teachings can be explained in simple, kindergarten style. Or they can be explained in much greater depth and detail, as in a theology course. You ought to keep studying these teachings; you should grow in your understanding of Catholic faith. But always keep in mind the simple, beautiful story that can be put in words so simple that a child can understand.

Put in simple terms—there is a God who made everything and who loves us. There is one God. There are three Persons in one God: the Father, the Son, the Holy Spirit; God the Son came to this world to save us. He was born, lived, suffered, died and rose from the grave. Jesus Christ, the God-man, started a Church so that His followers could carry on His memory and teachings. We show in life, then, how thankful we are — by believing what God tells us is true and by doing what God tells us to do.

But for adults, a list of the main truths is needed. There is an "old" list called the Apostles' Creed. A similar Creed, dating from 325 A.D., is recited at every Sunday Mass. So it is easy to find and to study the main Catholic teachings.

In 1971 a "General Catechetical Directory" was published by the Vatican. It gives a handy listing of the main teachings. The U.S. Bishops also have been at work to draw up a list of fundamental teachings.

I shall list for you these 25 basic teachings. If you are not Catholic and are studying the religion, these teachings will have to be explained in more detail by someone who knows Catholic faith. If you are a Catholic, this list can well serve as a checklist or punch list. If after each one you can honestly say "Yes," then you are well on the way to understanding Catholic faith.

1. THERE IS ONE GOD — FATHER, SON, HOLY SPIRIT.   The Holy Trinity is a mystery. We believe it because God has said it is so.
2. WHILE LIVING IN THIS SECULARIZED WORLD, WE MUST KNOW, LOVE AND SERVE GOD. We are helped to do this by worship in the Mass.
3. WE MUST CONTINUE TO STUDY THIS FAITH. Each of us must live the faith, and by our works show that our faith in Christ is genuine.
4. JESUS CHRIST, SON OF GOD, WAS BORN, WAS OBEDIENT UNTO DEATH. By His Resurrection, Jesus Christ brings us salvation and a new life.
5. GOD CREATED THE UNIVERSE OUT OF NOTHING. This creation was the beginning of the "history of salvation" of men through Jesus Christ.

6. JESUS CHRIST IS THE CENTER AND THE FULFILLMENT OF GOD'S PLAN TO SAVE MEN.

7. JESUS CHRIST, TRUE MAN AND TRUE GOD, LIVED IN SUCH A WAY AS TO SHOW US HOW TO LIVE AND PRAY AND HELP OTHERS IN LIFE.

8. JESUS CHRIST IS SAVIOR AND REDEEMER OF THE WORLD. By His most holy death, Jesus redeemed mankind from the slavery of sin and of the devil.

9. IN THE CHURCH WE ARE UNITED WITH GOD IN CHRIST. The sacraments are signs of grace which produce grace. The sacraments are actions of Christ in the Church.

10. THERE ARE SEVEN SACRAMENTS. EACH ONE IS DIFFERENT. Each one, by the will of Christ, produces grace. A person must have the right intention to receive the sacrament worthily.

11. THE SACRAMENTS ARE BAPTISM, CONFIRMATION, PENANCE, EUCHARIST, HOLY ORDERS, MATRIMONY AND ANOINTING OF THE SICK.

12. THE EUCHARIST IS THE CENTER OF ALL SACRAMENTAL LIFE. Christ is really present in the Eucharist under the appearances of bread and wine. The Eucharist is a sacrifice which nourishes us with Christ.

13. IN THE MODERN WORLD SPECIAL ATTENTION MUST BE GIVEN TO MATRIMONY AS A SACRAMENT.   Christian faith demands respect for the sacredness and indissolubility of Matrimony, for God's laws concerning procreation, and for the values of family life.

14. IN CHRIST I AM LIVING A NEW LIFE—A LIFE OF GRACE. The Holy Spirit in my soul works to overcome weaknesses and to bring strength and virtues.

15. MY LIFE IS GIVING TO GOD A FREE RESPONSE FOR ALL THAT JESUS CHRIST HAS DONE. Man should always be free.

16. SIN IS AN OBSTACLE: ORIGINAL SIN, SERIOUS ACTUAL SIN, OTHER OFFENSES AGAINST GOD. As a sinful person I must, with the graces of Christ, liberate myself from sin.

17. MY MORAL CODE IS A PERSONAL RESPONSE TO LIFE IN CHRIST. My response is readiness to keep all the Com-

mandments of God, all the Church laws and just civil laws. In morality, the Church is our guide.

18. A MORAL CODE IS BASED ON LOVE OF GOD AND LOVE OF NEIGHBOR. Morality is positive and not negative.

19. THE SOUL OF OUR MORALITY IS THE OBLIGATION OF CHARITY AS THE "NEW COMMANDMENT." We are to follow a way of life in which love is the prevailing spirit as we keep the commandments.

20. THE CHURCH, THE NEW PEOPLE OF GOD, IS GOD'S PLAN AND WAS INSTITUTED BY CHRIST. This is the Catholic Church which in the Holy Spirit teaches and guides us infallibly.

21. THE CHURCH IS UNIFIED. ALL IN THE CHURCH ARE EQUAL IN DIGNITY, AND ARE EQUALLY RESPONSIBLE FOR STRENGTHENING THE CHURCH.

22. THE CHURCH IS IN THIS WORLD AND WORKS TO BENEFIT SOCIETY. But the Church, as God's instrument for the redemption of all, is above this society.

23. THE BIBLE IS GOD'S INSPIRED MESSAGE TO MEN. The Bible is to be honored and read. It is to influence our daily living and our understanding of the liturgy.

24. MARY, VIRGIN MOTHER OF THE LORD, IS OUR SPIRITUAL MOTHER. We honor the saints, and in a special and personal way we venerate the Blessed Mother.

25. AFTER DEATH EVERY MAN WILL BE JUDGED BY GOD. I believe in heaven, hell, purgatory, and in the final judgment after Christ comes again at the end of the world.

This is a long list, but a helpful list, of the main teachings of Catholic faith.

On Keeping Sunday Holy

It is helpful to think about the approach to Sunday which any follower of Jesus Christ should develop.

These ideas and suggestions are not about Sunday Mass, but rather Sunday apart from Mass. About what a Catholic or any Christian is to do on Sunday besides attending Mass.

Many baptized people, I suspect, do not know what is so special about Sunday. They do not know the story behind the calendar, and why this day is set down as the first day of the week.

It is remarkable that, with all the thought of renewal in the Church and with many trying to live a thoroughly Christian life, little is said or thought of one of the oldest of religious principles: honoring the Sabbath day. Here is the third of the ten commandments, imposed partly to give God honor but also to satisfy the needs of man.

There is a rhythm to nature and to human life. In that human ecology the Sabbath is of enormous importance. Without one day of rest in seven, a man plays havoc with his natural and supernatural machinery. The precise day of the week may vary — for the Mohammedans it is Friday; for the Jews, Saturday; for the Christians, Sunday. But the basic need for one special day of rest and holiness is clear.

The Sabbath touches on the fundamental rules for balanced, sane living. We are to live in harmony with God's laws and with our fellow men; to live in harmony with all nature—with the earth's weather, its plants, tides, air, matter and creatures. To do this—to do it wisely and harmoniously—a Sabbath day is necessary every week. The person who observes the Sabbath will be better integrated, happier, more at peace.

The eighth day

For the follower of Jesus Christ, the Sabbath is that day of the week on which the Lord rose from the dead. So the Christian Sabbath, then, is not just a day of rest and re-creating oneself. It is the weekly holy day; it is a "little Easter."

The beauty and importance of Sunday have been well described by the Second Vatican Council. These words should express your personal views on the meaning of Sunday.

> "By an apostolic tradition which took its origin from the very day of Christ's resurrection, the Church celebrates the paschal mystery every eighth day. With good reason this, then, bears the name of the Lord's day or the day of the Lord. For on this day Christ's faithful should come together into one place so that, by hearing the Word of God and taking part in the Eucharist, they may call to mind the passion, the resurrection, and the glorification of the Lord Jesus, and may thank God who 'has begotten us again, through the resurrection of Jesus Christ from the dead, unto a living hope' (1 Peter 1, 3). Hence the Lord's day is the original feast day, and it should be proposed to the piety of the faithful and taught to them in such a way that it may become in fact a day of joy and of freedom from work" (Constitution on the Liturgy, N. 106).

That description of Sunday as the "eighth day" is interesting and instructive. I recall when this idea appeared in the Latin text under discussion at the Council in Rome. To look at each Sunday as "every eighth day" takes us back

"There is a rhythm to nature and to human life. In that human ecology, the Sabbath is of enormous importance."

in thought to the first day in this cycle: that day when Christ rose from the tomb, on the first day of the week and the first Christian Sabbath.

How to observe Sunday

Those of us nurtured on the Baltimore catechism received thorough instruction on observing Sunday. We were taught to attend Mass—and we were taught the necessity of avoiding all unnecessary servile work on that day.

In 1973, however, the United States bishops set down the duties expected of a Catholic Christian. It is quite instructive to note the positive way in which the Sunday obligation is stated in "Basic Teachings for Catholic Religious Education."

The bishops set down as the first of seven external manifestations of a genuine Catholic life the following: "To keep holy the day of the Lord's Resurrection: to worship God by participating in Mass every Sunday and Holy Day of Obligation; to avoid those activities that would hinder renewal of soul and body, e.g., needless work and business activities, unnecessary shopping, etc."

This is a far more positive expression of the Catholic view on Sunday. It avoids the complicated question as to what is servile work and what is not. It says that Sunday is to be a day of renewal of soul and body—so that we must avoid working as usual, business as usual and anything else that would spoil the sacred, re-creative meaning of this day.

How to sanctify Sunday

With the pattern of busy, pressurized modern living, how should a person go about keeping this day holy? There are several recommendations that I offer you.

FIRST RECOMMENDATION: Wear your best clothes. Our entire religious tradition holds that this is a special day, the Lord's day, a day of culture and renewal. This belief should be expressed by the way we dress, all day long. We put on our best clothes to visit God's house, and we stay reasonably well dressed throughout the remainder of the day. The individual Catholic who does not dress up for Sunday is a person who really does not understand the full meaning and importance of the "every eighth day." Somehow the very fact that we wear our "Sunday best," our "Sunday-go-to-Meetin'-clothes," says something to ourselves and to others — something about the quality of our personal religious life and observance.

The current trend to informal dress should not be reflected in the Christian reverencing the Lord's day. Yet all of us have had to see some extraordinary sights on Sunday in Church — clothing ranging from the sloppy to the exhibitionistic — which indicate that the wearer is sadly deficient in knowing the meaning of the Lord's day as well as the meaning of worship in the Lord's house.

What clothing should one wear on Sunday? This is the day of the week for your more formal attire. Men should dress in suitcoat, collar and tie. Women should dress in unostentatious, modest, quality fashion. And throughout the entire day, one's clothing should express an appreciation of the importance of that day. Let your clothing speak of your religious convictions.

SECOND RECOMMENDATION: Bring out your religious values on the Lord's Day. The ideal Sunday is one spent in re-creating one's highest and best values. Should it happen that you have had to shorten your personal prayers or devotions during the week, now you have a chance to make this up in your private devotions.

This is, of course, an ideal day for family prayer. An excellent tradition is "hearing" the children — at breakfast or at dinner, asking each of them to repeat as much of the homily as is remembered. This is the proper day to visit shrines. This is the day when many groups within the Church are able to have days of recollection, spiritual sessions, prayers in common, etc. Though Sunday Vespers are now not usual, the idea of special Sunday prayers remains a cherished Catholic tradition.

THIRD RECOMMENDATION: Make Sunday your day of culture. Because this is a day to renew your life, this is the best day to develop those cultural values which have been lost in the lives of many. This is a day for literature and the arts. For self-education. For visiting places of historical and cultural value. It is helpful to have around the house extra decorations on the Lord's day, especially at the table. It is fitting to follow a different meal schedule on this day, if that is feasible.

FOURTH RECOMMENDATION: Make Sunday a day of leisure and recreation. It has been noted many times that modern Americans do not know how to relax. When they have leisure time, they cannot enjoy a moment's rest. For many Americans, leisure time has taken the place of work and has also acquired most of the attributes of work — so that leisure brings no re-creation from within but rather more tiredness of body, mind and soul. This is the "weekend syndrome," the "Sunday neurosis" that have made leisure an exhausting problem for many who cannot remain still because they have to be enjoying themselves.

Sunday should be the day of genuine rest and healthy recreation. Retirement is becoming a factor in the lives of many. Sunday should be one's preparation for retirement, one's day for the higher values in living. This is the day to stroll rather than to ride, to play a game rather than watch a game on TV, to enjoy silence and peace.

A prayer that many Americans need to say and follow has been credited to Cardinal Cushing of Boston. It goes: "Slow me down, Lord! Ease the pounding of my heart by the quieting of my mind. Steady my hurried pace with a vision of the eternal reach of time. Give me, amid the confusion of the day, the calmness of the everlasting hills...Teach me the art of taking minute vacations — of slowing down to look at a flower, to chat with a friend, to pat a dog, to read a few lines from a good book. Remind me each day of the fable of the hare and the tortoise, that I may know that the race is not always to the swift — that there is more to life than increasing its speed.... Slow me down, Lord, and inspire me to send my roots deep into the soil of life's enduring values that I may grow toward the stars of my greater destiny."

This is a prayer that we can apply to life, yes, and also to our way of keeping Sunday holy. Slow me down, Lord.

FIFTH RECOMMENDATION: Do not shop or work on Sunday, if you can possibly avoid it. From all that has been written, it is clear that, for the Christian, buying and selling on the Sabbath is abhorrent and irreligious.

The Founding Fathers and pioneer politicians of all the original colonies had strict laws requiring church attendance and banning work, travel, sports and commerce on Sunday. In the 17th Century such regulations were written on blue paper, and they are still referred to as "blue laws." The courts in the United States, and recently the Supreme Court, have ruled on the necessity of one legal day of rest a week, and so have established the Sabbath as one of the civil institutions of the States.

Since the 1950's there has been constant pressure to repeal or relax these laws. As the courts and labor unions have pointed out, a day of rest is important. For the genuine Christian, however, there is no "business as usual" on Sunday, primarily because of religious reasons. The Catholic who buys or sells or works unnecessarily on Sunday is destroying the sanctity of this day and is giving the worst of example. As Pope John wrote: "It is with great sorrow that we note and deplore the ever-increasing neglect of, if not downright disrespect for, this sacred law."

The vigil Mass problem

Catholics who habitually attend Sunday Mass at the Saturday Vigil may be setting the stage for a spiritual problem. The problem is not the discernable tendency to dress informally at this time. The problem concerns the responsibility to keep the Lord's day holy in the way described in this instruction. Mass attendance is part of our Sunday observance. I have been told of individuals who regularly attend the Vigil Mass, consider that they have fulfilled their duty, and then do their washing and shopping on Sunday.

The Vigil permission was granted for those who were finding some difficulty in Sunday Mass attendance. If you have a free choice between Sunday morning and Saturday evening, choose Sunday morning. But if you do make use of the Vigil Mass, by all means dress for Sunday Mass and on the next day proceed to keep the Sabbath, the Lord's Day, in such fashion that you renew your spirit, mind and body.

The importance of keeping Sunday holy

Those of us who believe in God and worship and who want a real Sabbath cannot rely on the legislature to do the whole job for us. A legislature can and should repel the invasion of commercialism. But a legislature cannot make the day holy.

This is the job for believers — and not too many are doing it well. There is no end of professed believers, nominal Catholics and Protestants and Jews, whose Sabbath is spiritually no different from any other day of the week. Whose Sabbath is no different indeed from that of a practicing atheist. They tumble out of bed into old clothes or sports clothing, putter around the back yard or beach all day or seat themselves before TV, or go out and crowd the highways. They do not turn their minds to God for a single instant nor utter a syllable of prayer, let alone go to Church. Sunday for such Christians has no character, no quality, no dignity, no distinction, no religious flavor, no hint of the sacred.

Our first job as believers, then, is to restore visibility to Sunday as a day of worship and renewal. And the ones to help in this are all believers. Not just those who practice the faith but those who profess to be Catholic — our many who are not now going to church and who rarely offer formal worship to God; those who hope to practice their religion vicariously by sending their children to instructions; those who want churches and schools to keep going but never support them; those who want a religious framework for society but who ignore God themselves and leave religion out of their daily lives completely.

The crumbling of Sunday in modern society should be a warning of how easily religion itself can fade. The unchurched majority who do not deny God should get back into their churches, not only to save Sunday but to save the religious quality of society. And those good and faithful servants of God who go to church should keep in mind the wisdom and importance, both personal and national, of keeping the Sabbath, and keeping it holy.

"Every Mass we join in, ideally,
means going through a familiar
journey which, though familiar,
is different and novel every time."

Practical Hints on
Participating in the Mass

Catholic living is intimately connected with faithful attendance at Mass on Sundays and Holy Days. Attendance at Mass is a barometer of a faithful and practicing Catholic.

Occasionally these days we may hear someone questioning the necessity of Sunday Mass. So many things, it is said, have been changed. Is it possible that the Sunday Mass tradition will be changed? Or that Catholics will be allowed to go on any day of the week? Or that there will be no obligation to go, but just an encouragement?

The answer to all these questions is "No." Far from disappearing as an outdated obligation, the Sunday celebration takes on greater importance in the light of the Second Vatican Council. We have all been baptized in Christ. We are, therefore, not alone. We are together in Christ's Mystical Body, the Church. And so we assemble — as did our ancestors in this faith — on the day of our Lord's Resurrection. To remember and to renew just as He told us to do. To read our sacred books and learn from them. To encourage one another in the Christian life. To celebrate His life, death and Resurrection. To share in the oneness of His Body and Blood. And it is precisely in the Sunday celebration of our parish that we come together to honor God in this highest form of prayer.

The Mass is a celebration. The Sabbath and the Sunday Mass should be, as the Vatican II Fathers said, occasions of "joy and freedom from work."

It is a good and necessary thing that the obligation to worship God publicly, formally, liturgically, should bind us. The obligation should be understood and interpreted in sensible fashion, of course. But a serious responsibility before God to gather every week on the Lord's Day at Mass is good for all members of the Christian community.

We need this regular worship to survive spiritually, just as we need Holy Communion to maintain spiritual life in us. The U.S. bishops have said: "We too must express in signs our faith in Christ and each other, our love for Christ and for each other, or they will die."

But going to Mass Sunday after Sunday simply from obligation—that is a pitiful state of affairs. It is better than not going at all, of course. But the solution is to adopt a more mature, more Christian, more Vatican II approach to Sunday and Holy Day Mass: to attend with alertness a ceremony that is meaningful because we understand it and actively participate in it.

The history of the Mass

This is the ancient ceremony that has been repeated again and again by the Church of Jesus Christ. Indeed, even before the cross was the sign of Christ's followers, the Mass existed. What happens in our Catholic churches today would have been familiar in all essentials to countless Christians for nineteen centuries—to the saints and sinners who have made up the company of Christians since God first took bread and broke it in a borrowed room in Jerusalem.

The Mass is the most simple and subtle act of worship. It has been loved and died for. It has been criticized, outlawed, rejected as idolatry. But it remains for the majority of Christians, in all its differing outward forms, the most important action they are capable of doing. This is the best form of worship that we have to offer — because it is the doing, the sacrifice, of Jesus Christ as well as of ourselves in union with Him.

The basic outline of the Mass has remained the same through the centuries. The Second Vatican Council called for a simplification of the ritual and permitted the Mass in the language of the people. The Mass, then, is just the same as it always was — but now is much easier to understand and to celebrate.

Before going to church

It is good to plan to arrive early for Mass. One of your reasons for selecting a particular Mass on the schedule, in fact, should be that you can get there without rushing, without being in danger of lateness, without having any compulsion to hasten away.

Arrive early — but not so early that you find the parking lot filled with cars from an earlier Mass. And if you can walk to church rather than ride, you will be even better disposed to worship with fewer distractions. Getting there about ten minutes before Mass is about right.

You are probably accustomed to dipping your fingertips in the holy water font and making the sign of the cross on yourself. This is a traditional reminder of your own baptism in Christ, and of the new sinless life in Christ that you are living — and exercising today with the Church community.

If the Blessed Sacrament is kept in your church (the sign is the tabernacle and a special "tabernacle light"), then you should genuflect before entering a pew. This is a formal gesture of respect to the Eucharistic Lord. You should do this deliberately, to show reverence, and should bend the knee before (or in the direction of) the Blessed Sacrament. As you genuflect, say a prayer of adoration.

Many Catholics at the present time genuflect in hasty, improper fashion. For some this gesture means nothing.

Others genuflect in the center, even when the Blessed Sacrament is to the side. Such individuals have need of a refresher course as to what the genuflection is, and how and why it is done. And if Mass is in an auditorium or location where the Blessed Sacrament is not present, you need only bow to the cross.

Where do you sit? Select a location which will give you the best opportunity for participation in the Mass. Usually the front quarter of the church is your best place for seeing, hearing and participating.

After entering the pew, kneel for a few minutes of prayer before sitting down. This is a valuable time for private prayer in the Lord's house. If you have not yet said morning prayers, this is an opportunity to express the familiar sequence of ideas: adoration, thanksgiving, acts of faith, hope and love, resolution to live in Christlike fashion and worship well.

Then it is time to prepare for the liturgy. Now you need help. A "missalette" may be in the pew, or a hand missal may be available. Usually these books explain the general theme or lesson of the day's Mass. Read the theme. If there is time, read the Scripture lessons — starting with the Gospel — and the prayers. This preparation will help you considerably to follow the Mass with attention and benefit.

The parts of the Mass

In talking or thinking about the Mass, first attention should be given to the Eucharistic Prayer. This, the center of the Mass, is that part when the Church recalls Jesus Christ, does again what the Lord did at the Last Supper, and prays with Him to the Heavenly Father. The Eucharistic Prayer is the heart of the Mass and deserves our close attention, our "Amen."

The Eucharistic Prayer is followed by the Communion Rite. Starting with the Our Father, we prepare for Holy Communion with our Lord.

Immediately before the Eucharistic Prayer is the short Offertory. Now the bread and wine, usually brought to the priest in a procession, are offered to God.

And before the Offertory there is a "Liturgy of the Word," when we listen to selected readings from the Bible and have them explained in the homily. At this time in the Mass, we review our sacred writings, our written heritage.

And before the Liturgy of the Word, there is a short Introductory Rite. In this we express our sinfulness and say together prayers to our God.

Every Mass we join in, ideally, means going through a familiar beloved journey which, though familiar, is different and novel every time.

The preparatory rites

After processing to the sanctuary and reverencing the Blessed Sacrament, the priest kisses the altar — because the altar represents the Body of Christ and is the sacred place of sacrifice.

During the procession you may join in a hymn. Then you receive an opening greeting from the priest. There follows a short penitential rite. At this time you should recall your own failures, sins, selfishness and pride — and should ask God's pardon and mercy with the help of the subsequent prayers.

If the "Gloria" is said, make this an expression of your praise of God. Then listen to the Opening Prayer of the Mass — and make its sentiments your own. This you do by saying "Amen" at its end.

The Scripture readings

This part of the Mass is controlled by a separate book, the "Lectionary for Mass." The Lectionary is a large book, usually kept open at the pulpit, from which the lectors and priest read Bible passages for the day's liturgy.

The Lectionary is a remarkable piece of work. In clever fashion it gives us Bible readings expressing the message of the Bible as well as the liturgical season. By paying close attention to the readings, Sunday after Sunday, an alert Catholic can become reasonably familiar with the entire Bible.

Every Sunday there are three readings. These are printed in the Lectionary in a three-year cycle. For example, the year 1987 brings readings from the A cycle; 1988 from the B cycle; 1989 from the C cycle; 1990 the A cycle again, etc.

During the ordinary green-vestment Sundays ("Sundays in Ordinary Time"), we have Gospel readings in somewhat continuous fashion. Cycle A has Matthew's Gospel; Cycle B that of Mark; Cycle C, Luke's. During Lent and Advent we read John's Gospel. Each time you stand for the Gospel, therefore, you are listening to another ongoing section of our most precious writings. And every three years you will have reviewed all four Gospels.

The first reading is generally from the Old Testament. This is chosen with two points in mind: (1) to illustrate some common link, some parallel, with the Gospel reading; (2) to acquaint us with all the 46 books of the Old Testament over the 3-year cycle. So you should listen carefully to the first reading for two reasons: to learn about this particular Old Testament book, and to notice the theme that will be picked up in the third reading, the Gospel.

After the Old Testament reading there is a "Responsorial Psalm." This is part of an Old Testament Psalm, chosen because it voices the sentiments of prayer we should express to God after hearing this first reading. There is a striking similarity in mood and sentiment between the Old Testament reading and the psalm which responds to it.

The second reading each Sunday is from the New Testament writings. Because of the parallel between the other readings, we might be tempted to pay less attention to this second reading. But it is important and helpful. This is simply a continuing reading from the New Testament. So Sunday after Sunday we go through the other books of the New Testament. It is interesting that every year we start the cycle by reading selections from Paul's First Letter to the Corinthians. This one letter is given emphasis because the concerns and questions of the Corinthians and the answers of Paul have perennial relevance for the Church today.

The Liturgy of the Word is designed as a class in Bible reading and Bible study. The homily—an explanation of the readings with a lesson for contemporary Christian living—is meant to help us in learning and living the Word of God for today.

The sermon or homily

The preferred term now is the homily—but most still refer to it as the sermon. Any faithful adult Catholic is a veteran of thousands of sermons—and probably has some rather definite ideas on whether sermons are good or bad, in general and also in his or her parish.

A particular problem today is that so many tend to measure sermons according to the standards of TV or radio. Such standards are unrealistic, as most of the people in the pews would admit if they were called upon to deliver a speech before an audience or before a TV camera. Both realism and Christian charity should dispose one to be sympathetic towards the priest or deacon who must preach to others.

This said, however, it is true that there is no substitute for a carefully prepared, practical sermon with a message that inspires and encourages us to live the Christ-life with greater courage and spirituality. A good sermon does help much. Even a poor sermon, however, always has good in it—if we listen carefully. The sermon is not the most important feature of the Mass. But it is important, and is never to be neglected.

The Eucharistic Prayer

This longer prayer is the "center of the entire celebration." Always introduced with a Preface, it is always concluded with a solemn "Amen." This is a presidential prayer, voiced by the priest alone. He is to try for clear, deliberate and warm delivery, following the exact words. Now the people are to listen attentively and put their "Amen" to it all.

The new Missal has a large number of prefaces — approximately 70 new ones. The preface is tailored to the specific liturgy of the Mass being celebrated.

There are four different Eucharistic Prayers. By now the alert Catholic has become acquainted with all of them. The first is the old Roman Canon, developed between the 5th and 7th Centuries and used exclusively in the Western Church from the 11th Century until recently. The longest of the four, it is the most structured. The second Eucharistic Prayer, the shortest, is an enlargement of the 3rd Century Apostolic Tradition of Hippolytus of Rome. It is simple and rich. The third Eucharistic Prayer, a modern work, is a shortened and simplified version of the Roman Canon. The fourth is the longest of the new texts, is perhaps the best of the Canons, and expresses recent biblical and catechetical developments.

The chief elements of the eucharistic prayer are these:

a) Thanksgiving (expressed especially in the preface): in the name of the entire people of God, the priest praises the Father and gives him thanks for the work of salvation or for some special aspect of it in keeping with the day, feast, or season.

b) Acclamation: united with the angels, the congregation sings or recites the "Sanctus." This acclamation forms part of the eucharistic prayer, and all the people join with the priest in singing or reciting it.

c) Epiclesis: in special invocations the Church calls on God's power and asks that the gifts offered by men may be consecrated, that is, become the body and blood of Christ and that the victim may become a source of salvation for those who are to share in communion.

d) Narrative of the institution and consecration: in the words and actions of Christ, the sacrifice he instituted at the Last Supper is celebrated, when under the appearances of bread and wine he offered his body and blood, gave to his Apostles to eat and drink, and commanded them to carry on this mystery.

e) Anamnesis: in fulfillment of the command received from Christ through the Apostles, the Church keeps his memorial by recalling especially his passion, resurrection, and ascension.

f) Offering: in this memorial, the Church — and in particular the Church here and now assembled — offers the victim to the Father in the Holy Spirit. The Church's intention is that the faithful not only offer the spotless victim but also learn to offer themselves and daily to be drawn into ever more perfect union, through Christ the Mediator, with the Father and with each other, so that at last God may be all in all.

g) Intercessions: the intercessions make it clear that the eucharist is celebrated in communion with the whole Church of heaven and earth, and that the offering is made for the Church and all its members, living and dead, who are called to share in the salvation and redemption acquired by the body and blood of Christ.

h) Final doxology: the praise of God is expressed in the doxology which is confirmed and concluded by the acclamation of the people.

All should listen to the eucharistic prayer in silent reverence and share in it by making the acclamations.

— from General Instruction of the Roman Missal

Daily Mass

One of the recent popes has said: "If we really understood the Mass, we would be there every morning." How true it is: blessed are those with enough common sense and time to participate in daily Mass, to receive daily the Lord's Body and Blood for strengthening their souls.

The Lectionary and the Missal make weekday Mass a daily lesson in the Scriptures and in the liturgical treasures of the Church. Therefore a weekday hand Missal is especially recommended for those attending daily Mass.

There are two readings for weekday Masses. The Gospel, a continuous reading, is carefully chosen to harmonize with the Sunday Gospels. The first reading is also continuous, and takes us through a two-year journey of the entire Bible. And these weekday Masses will acquaint us with the rich variety now in the liturgy — the occasional memorials or feasts of saints, the various votive Masses and prayers of the faithful, the brief homilies, the shifting moods and feelings and understandings. All this makes possible a constant variety in the weekday liturgies — a variety that opens up the entire Bible and the fullness of our liturgy. This makes for a Catholic life strengthened each day by God's Word, by the Lord's Blessed Sacrament and the Church's beautiful liturgy.

When Sunday Mass Is Impossible

The faithful Catholic assigns highest importance to community worship of God on every Sunday and Holy Day. We are more than individuals. We are the People of God. Together with others we worship God. By participating in Mass we strengthen our sisters and brothers in Christ.

There may come times in your life, however, when going to Sunday Mass is impossible. Over a weekend you may find yourself in an isolated location where, in spite of searching, no Catholic Church or priest can be located. Or you may be hospitalized for a lengthy period. Or the limitations of age, or of the weather, may prevent you from leaving home.

What should you do on Sundays and Holy Days when it is impossible to get to Mass? By all means you should still worship God, since it is the Lord's Day. Worship God — and make your worship as liturgical as possible under the circumstances.

In many areas, Sunday Mass for shut-ins is available on television or radio. This will help you considerably in worshiping God, even though you are separated from the parish community.

A second helpful approach is to use a missal Go through the following steps:

1. Place yourself (or the entire group) in God's presence on this Lord's Day.
2. Say the Penitential Rite of the Mass to express sorrow for your sins.
3. Say the "Glory to God" in praise of the Holy Trinity.
4. Read attentively the three Scripture readings. Think how they relate to your life.
5. Say the Creed, the standard of your belief.
6. Pray for the special intentions—of the church, of the nation, of mankind, for the faithful departed, etc.
7. Say the Our Father.
8. Close with a final prayer to the Blessed Mother.

Because it has been impossible for you to attend Mass with the Community—and you have done the best under the circumstances—you should not make this a matter of Confession.

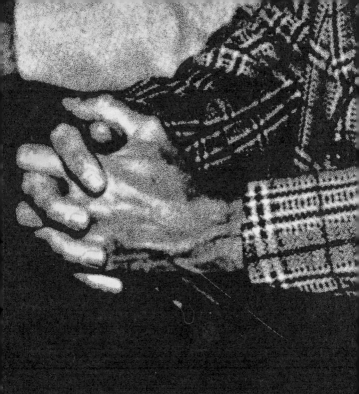

"What should you do
when Sunday Mass is
impossible? By all
means you should still
worship God, since it is
the Lord's Day—and
make your worship as
liturgical as possible...."

Practical Ideas on Confession

It is surprising how, as the years of life move on, we can develop our own ideas in regard to Church teachings. It is beneficial, therefore, to review from time to time the basic teachings of the faith.

It is indeed helpful to recall the importance of leading a sacramental life; in particular, how to make the most of Confession and Communion.

The sacrament of Confession

Most Catholics do not like to go to Confession. For many, this is much like going to the dentist — a painful duty which weak human nature tries to postpone as long as possible.

The theology of Confession

Why does the Catholic Church insist on this unpopular sacrament? Because this sacrament is the plan of Jesus Christ. And because it is a powerful, even necessary help for the Christian life. Jesus regarded sin as so serious that He died for the forgiveness of sins. John the Baptist pointed out Jesus as "the Lamb of God that takes away the sin of the world." And after His resurrection the Lord breathed over the apostles (a sign of giving the Holy Spirit), and told them to forgive sins or to withhold forgiveness with an authority that reached into heaven (look at St. John's Gospel, Chapter 20).

The ideal Catholic life, then, makes full use of Christ's plan for forgiving sins. The careless Catholic neglects this sacrament, usually to his or her spiritual harm. The prudent Catholic takes advantage of this sacrament by going regularly—and the spiritual benefits are enormous.

Confession is not really a painful procedure. For those who do go regularly it is a pleasant encounter with the merciful, forgiving Father.

The benefits of Confession

From the natural and supernatural viewpoints there are many benefits from a single confession. There is the "examination of conscience"—thinking over what you have done against God's Will, your habits of sin, specific sins and dangers, etc. Such a review is in itself a considerable help to right living. Then there is the "resolution of amendment"—a formal promise to God and yourself to seriously try to eliminate these sins and to avoid any occasions of sin. This in itself is enormously beneficial.

Then there is the action of confessing sins. This is an honest, sincere, humble admission that you are a sinner, that you indeed have sinned and have offended God and man. There is considerable therapeutic value, healing power, in just this. The proud person cannot admit this—and that is the weakness, the undoing of the proud person. There is the benefit of receiving personal advice from a wise, experienced spiritual counsellor. A prudent confessor is of immeasurable help to thousands of people, guiding them along the narrow path of holiness.

But the greatest benefit is the actual forgiveness of these sins by the priest of Jesus Christ. The load can be

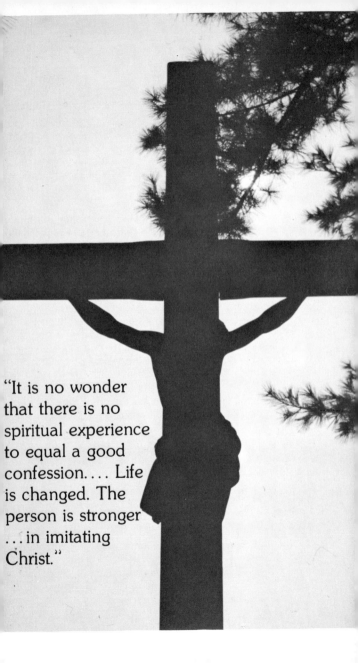

"It is no wonder
that there is no
spiritual experience
to equal a good
confession.... Life
is changed. The
person is stronger
...in imitating
Christ."

lifted off—and it is. The sins can be forgiven, on earth as in heaven—and they are.

It is no wonder that there is no spiritual experience to equal a good confession, properly made, fittingly celebrated, well accepted. The prayers of penance are said. Something is different. Life is changed. The person is stronger and sharper in identifying sin and temptation, in imitating Christ, in growing in grace and holiness.

A single confession is of immeasurable value and help. How sad it is that many Catholics neglect this needed, available means of grace. Those who need it most neglect it the most.

Do you commit sins?

The loss of a sense of sin is a fearful danger in modern living. Yet the loss of a sense of sin is common today, even in the lives of women and men given an education in Catholic religious values. The reason for this is that sin can be understood only by looking at it from the viewpoint of God. Sin is opposition to God. A sealing off of oneself from the love and will of God. A rejection of the love that the Father has shown to us in Jesus Christ. Sin is separation—separating man from God, from his neighbor, and from himself.

The problem today is that the spirit of the world makes people self-centered. So they cannot view sin from God's viewpoint. St. Anselm calls the sinner "a man twisted in upon himself." Today an individual can be completely self-centered, inconsiderate of others, living a lifestyle that neglects God's commandments, Christ's way and the Church's precepts—and still fancy himself as quite sinless. And this attitude is undoubtedly the greatest of his or her sins.

The late Evelyn Waugh, a convert, wrote perceptively of sin in his novel "Brideshead Revisited." A Catholic woman, living in a state of sin, was trying to stifle her conscience. One day she could hold back no longer: "All in one word, too, one little, flat, deadly word that covers a lifetime. 'Living in sin'; not just doing wrong...knowing it is wrong, stopping doing it, forgetting. That is not what they mean...Living in sin, with sin, by sin, for sin, every hour, every day, year in, year out. Waking up with sin in the morning, seeing the curtains drawn on sin, bathing it, dressing it...giving it a good time, putting it to sleep at night with a tablet of Dial if it's fretful."

Mortal and venial sins

The well-instructed Catholic keeps well in mind the difference between mortal and venial sins. This is most important for a clear, correct conscience.

Jesus Himself taught that all sins are not equally serious. A person commits a mortal sin when, deliberately refusing God's Will, he freely and with full knowledge acts against an important obligation of right living. By committing a mortal sin a baptized person loses the friendship of God. A mortal sin, then, is a terrifying reality: the breaking of one's relationship with God. And in order to commit a mortal sin, three factors must simultaneously be present. It must be 1) a serious matter, 2) done with sufficient, clear knowledge, 3) with full consent of the will.

There are other offenses, less serious, which we call venial sins. In certain cases it may not be easy for us to tell with certainty whether a sin is mortal or venial—because there can be excusing circumstances. Heredity, upbringing, education, social circumstances, public opinion, etc., may influence a person. A person may not realize that something is gravely sinful. Also, people often act without thinking. Or they react emotionally. Because God alone knows, we should leave this up to His mercy. But we should never be so foolish as to deny the reality of sin, or to try to rationalize our way out of a selfish, sinful act. In humility and in truth, we are all sinners.

How often is too often?

Occasionally I hear from disillusioned Catholics who have been scolded by the priest in Confession. The rebuke was caused not by the degree of their personal sins, but by the frequency of their "devotional" confessions. I too am shocked when confused, tearful penitents seek help after such harsh treatment. These were not scrupulous individuals misusing the sacrament. But rather just normal, concerned Christians who wish to advance in holiness and who believe that frequent confession can help them in that struggle.

I do not wish to exaggerate this complaint. Confession has suffered by abuses on both sides of the screen — but mainly, I believe, from the side of the penitent. It is quite wrong to think that frequent, devotional confessions are "out." The most recent ruling from the Holy See shows that they are "in," just as they have always been.

How often should a person go to Confession? Generally, this sacrament is necessary whenever one has seriously sinned against God and neighbor, or whenever God's Spirit points to a change of heart. Such a conversion — or "metanoia," or change of heart — should take place minimally during Lent and Advent. It also should occur at the start of any new state of life — confirmation, marriage, ordination, new occupation, new school, move to a new city, etc. It should happen whenever one takes part in an event aimed at a change of heart — a retreat, starting a school year, starting a vacation. It also should happen when a person feels that life is becoming a rut, that one is becoming careless or lazy or materialistic.

A Catholic who uses Confession at these times is making excellent, positive use of the sacrament. But what of setting up a regular pattern for yourself? The noted theologian, Karl Rahner, thinks that Confession once a month is a fair guide for serious-minded Christians. This indeed is a traditional Catholic pattern, as is shown by the confession opportunity before every First Friday. Some confessors will urge some penitents to approach the Sacrament about four times a year, in accord with the Ember Day tradition of reconciliation.

A practical ideal, however, is monthly confession. But the Catholic who has a problem with serious sin and who delays Confession until Easter or Christmas—that Catholic is simply not handling this Sacrament properly.

The Penance rite

A new ritual for this Sacrament was issued in Rome on February 7, 1974. It is a 121-page book, developed to carry out the 1964 ruling of the Second Vatican Council that the rites for all seven sacraments be revised and updated.

What is "new" in this present Penance Rite? What is different for the confessing Catholic? We are now encouraged to call this "Penance" or the "Sacrament of Reconciliation" because confession of sins is only a single step in the sacrament. There is an improved formula to be used by both penitent and priest, emphasizing reconciliation with God and with the Church.

The instructions on communal celebration of penance (with individual confession and individual absolution as the rule), the encouragement of devotional confessions, the allowing of a face-to-face celebration in addition to the private confessional—these are nothing new.

Practical hints

There are several common-sense ideas to keep in mind. Be strict and exact with yourself about celebrating this Sacrament of Reconciliation regularly. You have a standing, regular appointment with your forgiving heavenly Father. Keep it.

Give yourself time to go through the steps carefully. Never rush through this Sacrament. Try using the seven capital sins as a basis to examine your record, to review your sins.

It is important to say an "Act of Contrition" before you enter the confessional. Some Catholic youngsters these days do not do this, do not even know an Act of Contrition, and may for lack of sorrow for sin, be receiving the sacrament invalidly.

Confess your own sins—not those of other people. Do not give needless details but do give numbers or totals for serious sins. Do not worry about shocking the priest. As has been said, asbestos ears come with the grace of priestly ordination. Do not hesitate to ask for help when confessing— indeed, this is always prudent in a difficult confession.

Practical Ideas on
Holy Communion

We Catholics believe that Holy Communion is receiving into ourselves the Lord Jesus. This belief is rooted in the New Testament (read St. John's Gospel, Chapter 6. Remember what Christ did and said at the Last Supper.) In a sense there is no possible closer union with Christ on this earth than at the time we receive Communion. It is the Lord, under the appearance of bread and wine, who comes to us.

The New Testament presumes that any follower of Jesus is fully converted to Christ, finished with sin, growing in grace. The normal pattern for a Catholic, then, is to receive this heavenly food every day you attend Mass. The entire last part of the Mass, in fact, is the Communion Rite. Only mortal sin should prevent you from receiving Holy Communion every Sunday, Holy Day of Obligation and all other days that you attend Mass.

If you do not or cannot receive Holy Communion (because you are not a Catholic, because you are married without the Church's approval, because of a state of serious sin or because you have not been leading a sacramental life), you should make a spiritual Communion at this time of the

Mass. In a spiritual Communion you ask the Lord to come to you spiritually, because you cannot now receive the Eucharist physically.

Non-Catholics are not to receive Communion at a Catholic Mass, because Communion calls for a unity of faith with all those present of the Christian community. Similarly, Catholics are not to receive the Eucharist in Christian Churches not in unity with the Bishop of Rome.

You should receive Holy Communion with deep devotion towards the Lord's eucharistic presence. The dangers of receiving Christ in an irreverent, unworthy manner were stated by Paul to the Corinthians (First Corinthians, Chapter 11)—and those dangers hold true today. Never lose your awe, your feelings of unworthiness, as you take under your bodily roof the greatest of spiritual gifts.

Prepare yourself for Holy Communion. Pay close attention to the Mass prayers. Continue with your own prayerful thoughts, first of preparation and then of thanksgiving. It is disturbing to see the thoughtless, automatic way in which some Catholic youngsters receive this Sacrament. In spite of their nervousness and short attention span, they need a good practical lesson on the correct way to receive the Lord.

To receive while kneeling is, generally speaking, a more devout, less hurried manner of reception. Many older people, however, find it easier to stand. The mental attitude is more important than the physical: at the Last Supper the Apostles received while reclining on couches.

A further observation is that the individual who distributes Holy Communion is only a minister. Ask only that the distributor be a good Christian, approved by the Church and respectful of the Lord's Body. Concentrate on Whom you receive, not who gives you Communion. Sometimes Catholics think it is a special privilege to receive from a bishop, or that it is objectionable to receive from a layman commissioned for this service. Think of the Lord rather than of the one distributing—and be sympathetic towards the diocese or parish that does not have enough priests to give out Holy Communion without some delay.

How to receive Holy Communion? Make it devout for yourself and both convenient and safe for the priest, deacon or extraordinary minister. Do not rush. Say "Amen" when you hear the words "The Body of Christ." Your "Amen" is an act of faith in the Real Presence. If you choose to receive Communion on the tongue, tilt back your head, open your mouth and extend your tongue slightly—all this is so the one distributing Communion can safely place the Sacred Host on your tongue. If your head is kept steady there is no difficulty. But it is very difficult when the recipient does not open his mouth sufficiently, does not extend his tongue, or (worst of all) starts to move his head away before receiving the Host.

Communion in the hand has been approved as an optional way to receive in the United States of America. This, the ancient way of receiving, was the only way during the first thousand years of the Church's history.

If you elect to receive Holy Communion in the hand, take special care to be reverent. Follow the parish pattern. Come forward at the proper time, hands folded to indicate reverence. If you are to receive while standing, make in advance of reception an external sign of reverence: a genuflection, a bow or a sign of the cross.

Then position your hands properly, so that the minister of Holy Communion will know your preference. Rest one hand on the other, palms up, hands of course uncovered. A right handed person should place right hand beneath the left. A left handed person should have the left hand beneath. Extend the hands, keeping them level and crossed.

Say your "Amen" (a profession of faith). When the Host is placed on your palm, step to the side if necessary, then remove the lower palm, take the Host with the thumb and index finger and give yourself Holy Communion. Consume any small particle that may be left. Then begin your thanksgiving and, with hands folded, return to your place to continue thanking the Lord.

How one receives is not important—so long as it is a reverent reception in a manner approved by the Church. It is whom we receive that is important. Neither way of receiving, then, is better than the other. And no Catholic is a better Catholic for receiving one way or the other.

Prayers of thanksgiving after Holy Communion are most important. A good prayer book or missal will offer such prayers. How disedifying it is to see someone leave Mass early, or to see and hear a churchgoer talk in distracting fashion on the way out. And conversely, how inspiring it is to see a Catholic remain after Mass to make a longer thanksgiving.

Putting Faith into Action

How does a Catholic <u>practice</u> the faith? In former years people described themselves by saying "I am a practical Catholic." That is, I am a Catholic who puts my faith into action.

Now in the years following the Second Vatican Council, what are the actions expected in the life of a practical Catholic?

No list of practices can describe the Christ-life of the Catholic follower of Jesus Christ. However, it is helpful to know and to explain certain practices which can sustain and express the faith of our fathers.

The practices are, generally speaking, in addition to the Precepts of the Church. These practices describe what we <u>should</u> do rather than what we <u>must</u> do. A list such as this might be helpful for teachers of religion, especially on the junior high and high school level.

The practice of the Catholic faith

DAILY PRACTICES:
— praying to God: every morning; every night; before and after meals.
— spending some time every day in private prayer and spiritual reading.

WEEKLY PRACTICES:
— making every Sunday a day of personal renewal: my personal observance of the Lord's Day of Resurrection.

— celebrating each Sunday the Liturgy of the Mass by worshiping with the Christian community.
— observing every Friday as a day of penance in memory of the Lord's Sufferings and Death on a Friday.

MONTHLY PRACTICES:
— celebrating the Sacrament of Reconciliation (Penance)
— expressing devotion to the Sacred Heart.
— showing special devotion to the Blessed Mother during May; practicing the devotion of the Rosary during October, etc.

YEARLY PRACTICES:
— making Advent a time of special spiritual preparation for Christmas (Bible study and reading; Advent devotions, etc.)
— making Lent a time of spiritual and penitential preparation for the Feast of the Lord's Resurrection (Lenten Devotions; Stations of the Cross; abstinence and fast; Holy Week Services, etc.)
— attending Masses and having Mass said on anniversaries of our faithful departed.
— making a retreat or mission.
— observing Forty Hours Devotions to the Blessed Sacrament.

LIFELONG PRACTICES:
— moving in one's prayer life towards contemplation.
— when life's schedule permits, attending Mass daily and saying the Liturgy of the Hours.

OTHER PRACTICES AND CUSTOMS:
— wearing and possessing crucifixes, crosses, medals, scapulars, etc.
— showing reverence to the Blessed Sacrament (genuflecting, bowing, keeping silence, etc.)
— sacramentals of the Church (holy water, candles, blessings, etc.)

"No list of
practices can
describe the
Christ-life of
the Catholic
follower of
Jesus Christ
—however, it
is helpful...."

Ideas on Parish Life

A basic idea of Catholic living concerns the parish. Your relationship to your own parish, to your own pastor — these are ideas of no small importance in Catholic life.

Is the parish outdated?

In the years following the Second Vatican Council, nearly every department of Catholic living has been inspected and evaluated — in the light of the Gospel, in the light of modern living. A few observers have been highly critical of the parish, suggesting that the parish has "seen its day," that a better way of caring for the people should be developed. In this critical age the parish also has been criticized as being too impersonal, too large. So the parish priest does not know his people and they do not know him.

The parish is criticized for not providing more inspiration to parishioners. It is said that there are many good, educated Catholic laity who could be leaders in Church renewal. But the parish does not provide the spark to ignite them into action for Christ and neighbor. And so the laity tend to be as anonymous as possible — not registering, not helping, not truly participating in parish life.

There indeed are stresses today in parish life, as any priest can testify. But the picture is similar to Chesterton's statement about Christianity itself. The parish has not been tried and found wanting. It has not really been given a fair trial in our day. In an age when one of every five families moves every year, when most movement is into suburbia, and when there is a growing shortage of priests, we can readily understand that there will be some strains on parish life.

I no longer hear serious criticisms of the parish as an institution. Nothing on the horizon suggests that the parish will become less important. It is the basic unit of Catholic life and will continue as such.

The parish makes much good sense. It is the level where you as a Catholic fit into the Church of Jesus Christ. Here is where the action is — and should be — for any healthy diocese, The parish means accountability of a definite priest or priests for certain definite souls. And the parish makes it possible for the individual Catholic to participate in building up the community that is necessary for the Church to exist. No man is an island, and no follower of Christ can go it alone.

Our challenge today is not to cast about vainly for a replacement of the parish, but rather to develop, through personal efforts, the full potential of Christian living that every parish contains.

What a parish is

What is a parish? Mention "parish" to most Catholics and they think of a set of buildings — perhaps a church and rectory, perhaps also a school and convent. Perhaps some Catholics think only of a particular priest or of a number of priests when they think of a parish.

This is a common misconception. And an unfortunate one. What is a parish? It is a defined geographical or territorial area, in which a priest is assigned to care for souls of people living in that area and in which the laity of the area have a special relationship to their own pastor. So, strictly speaking, a parish could exist without any buildings at all.

"Our challenge today is...to develop, through personal efforts, the full potential of Christian living that every parish contains."

The parish is a venerable institution. In the days of the Apostles there were no parishes — no St. Abraham's in Jerusalem or St. John's in Ephesus. The first unit was the diocese, and priests assisting the bishop had no territorial area of responsibility. But by the 5th Century persecutions were over. The faith was being carried out into the countryside. Then parish boundaries were drawn and local pastors appointed. So the parish as an institution is over 1,500 years old.

In Europe the parish church was often the center around which villages and towns developed. It was different in the United States, especially along the Atlantic Seaboard. Here towns and cities grew around factories, railroad junctions, harbors, etc. The bishop established territorial parishes whenever and wherever the number of Catholics and the number of priests made it possible. But a special situation developed among great numbers of immigrants who needed and wanted to retain their own language and traditions in worship, their own priest, their own parish. So, many "nationality parishes" were established. Churches were built in the neighborhood where the immigrants lived. within walking distance.

Such is the background of today's parish scene. Then, as people moved to the suburbs, new parishes were established. But there is a special challenge now in the inner-city parish, territorial as well as national.

I am constantly surprised by the considerable difference from one parish to another. Each is a living unit, with its own history and traditions, its spirit, its type of buildings. Two parishes side by side can be as different from one another as sometimes members of one family differ from one another.

What to expect from your parish

The parish is a community of believers in which you have an appointed, reserved place. What should any Catholic expect in the parish and from the parish priests?

The Catholic follower of Jesus Christ expects to live a sacramental life in accord with the wisdom and rules of the Church. The parishioner, consequently, should expect sacramental service. A convenient opportunity to worship God in community on Sundays and Holy Days. Opportunity to celebrate the sacrament of Reconciliation or Penance. Help in education of children in the faith. A ready response to requests for Baptism, Marriage, the Anointing of the Sick and Christian burial.

These are the services which a Catholic should expect in the parish. These are the very services which a pastor is obligated by Canon Law to provide for the parishioners.

But as parish priests know so well, administering a parish effectively in contemporary America calls for much more. The liturgy must be carefully planned, with true participation and variety. The homily must be relevant to Scripture and to modern living. The educational program must be well planned, well supervised, especially today when at times parents are not practicing and transmitting the faith as they should.

There must be an ongoing encouragement of devotional and prayer life — devotions to the Blessed Sacrament, retreats, missions, Marian devotions, Lenten and Advent devotions. There should be a program for adult education in the faith.

And there should be a thrust beyond parish limits to the wider community. Programs of social service to others, of strengthening and helping the poor of society, ever with us in spite of governmental programs. There should be concern for Christian unity, shown by ecumenical involvement.

All this is a high ideal, beyond the effort of priests alone. That is why a parish council is desired — to advise the priests, to assist them towards these high goals of a living and vigorous parish. A parish council which knows its role and which has a truly Catholic view of Church and parish — such a council can be a blessing to a priest who is called upon to accomplish so much for the parishioners.

What your pastor should expect

Amidst the confusion of the past several years there has developed, in the thinking of some, particular confusion about the obligations of a parishioner towards the parish priest. According to our tradition and canonical regulations, this is a two-way street: the pastor has responsibilities toward the parishioner, and the parishioner also has certain responsibilities toward the pastor — and towards the other parishioners.

The pastor should expect that you as a parishioner see the parish not as his property, his worry, his thing — but as yours just as much as his. Probably the most general mistake in the contemporary Catholic Church is looking at the Church not as the People of God. The mistake of "looking up" all the time when thinking of the Catholic Church — as if the Church were the Pope's, the diocese were the bishop's and the parish were the priest's. The best picture of the Church and of the parish? The best picture is seen by looking in a mirror.

Every pastor ought to have the consolation that the laity shares the responsibility for it all. But the sad reality is that only a percentage have the correct, mature attitude towards the parish. Over and over again the priest is given the viewpoint that the parish is his, that seemingly he is the only one to carry the burdens. This happens when a Catholic moves into a parish and neglects to register. When a Catholic parishioner comes in to arrange for a baptism or marriage or funeral, and comes in as a stranger. When a Catholic resists using envelopes or (what is worse) refuses support to the parish. When a Catholic family benefits from a Catholic school but does not show any appreciation. Or when parishioners attend Mass elsewhere, or (what is worse) do not attend Mass at all on Sundays and Holy Days. The number is legion, and often the pastor feels isolated.

What should a pastor expect of a parishioner? First, registration. The mature, well-instructed, sincere Catholic sees to it that the family is registered at the rectory. This is quite important, considering the mobility of contemporary Americans. Be registered; be known. And if you move away, inform the parish secretary and say goodbye to the priests who have served and helped you.

Secondly, involvement. Your personal growth and parish growth are interrelated. Few grow religiously by themselves; there are not many holy hermits on the parish scene. Most Christians need to draw strength from their fellow Christians. And so, as the parish community sustains you, you should try to return the favor.

Your involvement in parish life may be influenced by factors which include these two: 1) What are the major needs, the priorities, of the parish? 2) What talents and services are you equipped to contribute? High on the priority list of every parish is the religious education of parish children. But Christian concern should not be directed only to the young — adults also need continuing religious education. The old and the sick deserve parish care. The poor need help. If the area is a changing neighborhood, the parish should react with the appropriate Christian response.

Thirdly, financial support is needed. This is a subject which Catholics, priests and laity, find distressing to discuss. The greatest cross of the priest is to have to mention finances from the pulpit. Here is where real faith and parish loyalty will be shown — in seeing to it that the priests do not have to worry about paying bills. Most parishes are perennially short of money — and if you have ever served as a collector at Sunday Masses, you know why.

A certain sympathy for the special collections should exist in your Catholic heart. We as a Church have special obligations flowing from the Gospel. Obligations to support the Pope, to help the poor in the underdeveloped countries, the poor in this nation, the missions, the underprivileged of the diocese, the struggling Catholic schools. I see these "second collections" as a Christian expression of our Gospel faith. We are in a sense privileged to share in these common efforts for Christ.

Shopping around for a parish

May a Catholic "shop around" for a parish — go about on Sundays from one church to another and then go regularly to one where the liturgy and sermons or some other aspect of parish life are more attractive? This is being done, as Catholics occasionally have told me — some without even knowing it is wrong; others with an expression of shame.

According to the Canon Law which binds us all, there is no possibility of transferring parish membership. One lives in a particular parish by virtue of residence. So geography, Church law, Baptism — all put you in your own parish. This makes good sense. You know who is obligated to give you the sacraments; you know where to go in times of need and illness. There are excellent practical reasons for this Church law.

It all seems so tidy, so neat. But there are unending problems in regard to this question. Problems caused by churches in too close proximity to one another, by personality conflicts, by vague parish boundaries, by Catholics either unacquainted with parish membership or simply unwilling for any reason to attend their own parish church.

In your Catholic life it may happen that you live near a school chapel, hospital chapel or religicus institution where Sunday Mass is offered for the religious or for employees. Should you start attending Masses there? As a general rule, no. You have a duty to your parish and parish community. If you attend an institutional Mass and neglect your parish, you are in some danger of offending against both justice and charity. And sooner or later you will run into difficulties, as on occasions when Church law requires a Catholic to approach one's parish.

It is a sensitive matter, especially in an age when "freedom" is the great watchword. But there is an ecclesial dimension to the way in which the Lord is to be worshiped: the Church, with its human weaknesses and limiting regulations, is still the Bride of Christ with power and authority and direction from God.

What about the Catholic who has good, serious reasons for going elsewhere for Sunday Masses? The approach is to talk over the situation with one's pastor and to follow his direction. Ordinarily speaking, difficult questions can be worked out without detriment to justice or charity.

The special, widespread problem is the Catholic unknown to his or her own pastor. My concern is that the anonymous Catholic can so easily become a non-practicing Catholic. Neglect of Church law can lead to neglect of divine law.

The nationality parish

Any treatment of parish life must make mention of the nationality parish. Not all parishes are territorial in the sense described above. Some parishes were designed to serve Catholics of a particular national origin. They have boundaries in a more general sense, in reference to the next parish for that specific national group.

For many such, blood lines have thinned as intermarriage has taken place among national groups. However, the nationality parish remains — to serve the children and grandchildren and new immigrants. The Catholic of a particular nationality descent has then the choice of belonging to the specific nationality parish, or the local territorial parish.

The inner-city parish

The movement to suburbia has created a special challenge: the inner-city parish. Once thriving with a large congregation, now it suffers most from high expenses and low resources. But some of the finest apostolic work is being done in such parishes, work for Christ and the community. The priests, sisters and laity of the inner-city parish have indeed special worries. But they have an opportunity to show the finest Gospel values in living the faith today.

Parish of the future?

The key to the future is spirituality. The real purpose of a parish is, in fact, to develop saints who praise God together, who as a community carry out the Two Great Commandments. The parish of the future is the one with its future based on spiritual values. Where prayer is taught and practiced during the week. Where the fallen-aways are visited and exhorted to return. Where there is a ministry to youth. Where the debts are paid, and the parish on principle helps poorer parishes. Where a spirit of cooperation, a family spirit, reaches out to all in the parish and beyond.

An impossible dream? No—but it will take some doing to reach that goal. It is the goal described in the Acts of the Apostles: the spirit of first generation Christianity.

Practical Hints For Praying

Suppose that you are a veteran in the Church—a veteran who can use an occasional check-up on daily Catholic living. Or suppose that you are an adult convert, anxious to do the Catholic job as well as possible. At any rate, suppose that you have a romance with Christ and the beautiful old Church of Christ.

It helps to think occasionally about your prayer life—especially your personal, private prayer. In modern times just as in ancient times, praying is an important, difficult, bothersome question for any follower of Jesus Christ. Yesterday, for example, did you pray? Did you say morning prayers? Night prayers? Meal prayers? Just how many minutes did you spend yesterday in talking with your God?

Probably any reader of these words is already dedicated to Christ and to the Catholic way of life and prayer. But there are many signs around us that neglect of prayer is widespread among Christians. Our Holy Father has complained that too many people today refuse to pray, if they ever think about it at all. A priest recently wrote: "Hardly enough prayer goes on among Catholics today to justify what they mean by prayer." A non-Catholic author has written of this same spiritual disease among Protestants. He says that "many Christians today, including many theologians, acknowledge that their prayer life is virtually nonexistent."

Any Catholic, any Christian not praying is failing as a follower of Jesus Christ. Prayer is the first obedient and loving response of a child of God to the heavenly Father. To be a Christian and to pray are one and the same.

And the person who does not pray is missing so much in life. Here is our assurance and insurance towards knowing God in heaven for all eternity. Real prayer is far better for us than any vacation, than any recreation. Prayer helps us to "put it all together" in life and to get it all pointed in the right direction. Prayer is our strength to hold ourselves together despite the experience of change within and outside ourselves. Prayer is our antidote against depression, our valid escapism into the peace of eternity, our self-realization, our expression of authentic personhood.

Why do Catholics not pray?

If prayer is so important, so helpful, why is it being neglected by so many? Pope Paul gave several reasons: lack of religious instruction, widespread denials of God, unbridled sensuality, an ever-growing human pride. To these we could add plain laziness and a disorganized pattern of living. Prayer is work—and no labor-saving device has yet been invented to do away with the work that prayer requires.

Many Catholics, I am convinced, just do not give praying a high priority in their lives. They may have hours of time each day for TV and radio, for recreation and eating and drinking. They may have time to waste. They may have time when they don't know what to do with themselves. But there is no time, say they, to pray.

Some Catholics do not pray because they have allowed their mental processes to be taken over by radio and television. Most adult Americans make their first mistake of the day right after they get out of bed. They turn on the news. This is a harsh way to start the day—with war, riots, killings, pollution, violence, hatred, crises. The list is endless.

Bad news, commercials, beat music—these are all destructive of tranquillity and prayer life. Constant emphasis

" 'Lord,
teach us to pray.'
Teach us to pray as adults."

on bad news can destroy our values, inhibit emotional growth, and increase depression. In Boston during a newspaper strike the suicide rate went down 22 per cent. When Seattle had no newspaper or TV, suicides there dropped 43 per cent. The wise person, consequently, controls the baneful influence of the media. The person who wants to pray must control the media even more carefully.

Pope Paul pointed out that a lack of religious instruction is to blame for many not praying. The problem among American Catholics is perhaps a lack of adult religious instruction. So many were taught prayers and praying habits as children — and probably in a much more settled society, with parents to give good example in adult praying. But for many contemporary Catholic adults, the parents have gone, and powerful and confusing sociological changes have swept across American society. And those orderly prayer habits of yesteryear have been lost amid all the noise, confusion and worry. Now many an adult Catholic has no real interior life — and stands defenseless before the strong temptations and silly ideas that are current today.

Somehow a refresher course in praying is needed today by most adult Catholic Americans. "Lord, teach us to pray" was the plea of the Apostles to Christ. The same plea is heard today from all sides. Teach us to pray as adults. As adults living in this noisy, confusing, troubled world. Put us in personal touch with our transcendent God, seven days a week.

Here are six suggestions for adult prayer in our times.

FIRST SUGGESTION: MAKE PRAYER IMPORTANT IN YOUR LIFE.

If you are really converted to Jesus Christ, then you have given over your entire life to Christ. And if that is true, then you will see your personal daily prayer life as of basic importance. Prayer will be at the top of your values in life, at the head of your daily agenda. But if you are not really dedicated to living in Christ, your prayer life will be weak.

Praying is most important for the follower of Christ because praying was most important for Christ. Our Master, as the Gospels make clear, used to go away from the crowd daily to pray to the heavenly Father. Before important decisions, the Lord used to pray through the entire night. He taught his followers the Our Father as a model of prayer, and told them to practice closing the door of their room and praying in secret to their heavenly Father. And Jesus taught and demonstrated how to pray during times of intense political crisis and social unrest in Palestine.

We should then have a positive outlook on prayer. It is based on a personal love for our good God. It is an appreciation of who God is and what God has done for us through Jesus Christ. So we view prayer in positive fashion, in reference to God. We do not view prayer from our own viewpoint only, as something that we sometimes find unpleasant, difficult, and then neglect to do.

SECOND SUGGESTION: MANAGE YOUR TIME.

It is true that we do the things every day that we consider important. And if we do not do them, we do not consider them as that important. So the person who puts daily prayer at the top of the day's agenda will make time for prayer. It is a question of priorities.

It is very easy to have time for prayer, even in the most hurried and harried life. In fact, the busy person is the one who most needs to develop good prayer habits. After a while even a busy person can develop techniques to pray at odd moments during the day, and even to pray when working or travelling. But the real prayer must be undistracted, when we close the door against the world and in tranquillity concentrate on God and talk with God. We can pray only when in a state of stability and inner peace, when we are face to face with God.

Most people feel tense, pressured, always behind schedule, rushed to do the jobs of life. A person in that state has no time or inclination to pray. And so he or she either does not pray, or prays quite distractedly.

To pray well we must master time. Not fearful of being alone with ourselves, we must stop the rush and be completely in the present moment. Our attitude must be like that of a person taking a walk on a holiday—we are not trying to get somewhere. We are content with what we are doing now, and we relish it to the full.

It is possible to exercise yourself in stopping time and remaining in peace in the present now. This ends the inner agitation, the fidgeting and worry, the clock-watching. Then you are master of time and can pray in peace in any storm— because the storm is always outside and not inside you.

How often each day should you try to do this? To make yourself completely still and poised in God's presence? A great theologian who lived 1700 years ago, Origen by name, said that a Christian should do this three times each day. I make the same recommendation to any adult Christian of this atomic age. Try to do this every day—at morning prayers, in your daily meditation, at night prayers.

THIRD SUGGESTION: YOUR MORNING PRAYERS.

Your first formal approach to God each day is of special importance. This sets the tone and direction of your whole day. When should you say morning prayers, and how should you say them?

If you have a satisfactory pattern developed, then by all means continue with what is working for you now. Each person must develop a personal approach for private praying—and the style of someone else will probably not work perfectly for you. Private prayer is like a home-made suit: you must make it for yourself, but you may use patterns and ideas from others.

I would recommend that you not say morning prayers immediately after rising, but wait until you have washed and dressed and cleared your mind of drowsiness. Be careful not to distract yourself with radio news and noise before your morning prayers are said. Then, just before the day's duties begin, sit yourself down or kneel down within view of a crucifix. Thinking out your own thoughts, go through the following six ideas:

1. Praise God (the "Glory be" or "Glory to God in the highest" may help)
2. Thank God for his goodness (for creation, for Jesus, for your Church, for parents, teachers, etc.)
3. An Act of Faith (Your Word, God, is the cornerstone of my intellectual life)
4. An Act of Hope (no matter what happens in society, my hope is in you, my God)
5. An Act of Love (the crucifix shows your love, God, for me)
6. A resolution to imitate Jesus Christ today.

That is all. It can be done in only a few minutes. But do it with calmness and gratitude to your loving Father in heaven. Let it start you on another day of balanced, holy, intelligent, efficient, calm living.

FOURTH SUGGESTION: YOUR DAILY MEDITATION.

Spiritual writers tell us it is most important to spend a longer period of time—say 15 minutes to a half-hour—in calm thought and prayer. This is the time when you look at the life and teachings of Jesus Christ and then at your own pattern of living. Without a daily meditation you will just run along through life and soon run down spiritually. You need this daily meditation to remind yourself every day of what you should be: another Christ in today's world.

Here again, you must develop your own approaches. I would recommend that you set aside your own time and place of prayer. Make it when your mind is most at peace. Many have learned to make meditation immediately after morning prayers, before the day's distractions start. Others do it before the evening meal...or before the noon meal...or in late afternoon.

The way to meditate is to put yourself in quiet and peace, and in the presence of God. Then think about Jesus Christ. Then think about how you are following that life and those teachings. Then make or renew your resolutions.

In meditating you can get much help from books. The Gospels contain the best food for thought. The "Imitation of Christ" will help you greatly. There are excellent publications from the Confraternity of the Precious Blood in Brooklyn—"My Daily Bread," "My Daily Life," "The Whole Story"—which you can get in a Catholic book store. And there are many other helps—meditation books, writings about the Blessed Mother, lives of saints, books of devotion.

As the years of life go by, this important prayer time becomes less concerned with self and more concerned with praising God and thinking of God in an uncomplicated fashion. This is contemplation, which gradually takes over all of one's thinking and living. But the fine art of contemplation is beyond our concern now.

If you set aside your time and place for daily meditation and then do it, you are trying to pray as you should.

FIFTH SUGGESTION: YOUR NIGHT PRAYERS.

As you began the day with prayer, so should you end it. Many Americans retire later than they should, and many end the day in distracted and tired fashion by watching or listening to the eleven o'clock news. There is little time or disposition left for either lengthy or original prayers.

So I would recommend the use of a prayer book for night prayers. Get some that you like, of a suitable length, and say them faithfully before going to bed. All night prayers should have a reference of self to God, gratitude for the day's graces, a short examination of one's performance that day, and a placing of self in God's care for the night. A lovely Catholic tradition is a final prayer to our Blessed Mother.

A lay Catholic could make daily good use of the official night prayer of the Church, or Compline. Or a Catholic could keep a Bible at bedside and say as part of Night Prayers Psalm 91, Psalm 86 or Psalm 16.

SIXTH SUGGESTION: HELPFUL HINTS ON PRAYING.

To learn to pray, a person should pray — that is, give the time to it and try it. Praying is like swimming. Instructions and suggestions help, but you must do it yourself and not just talk about it.

Try to remember how important it is to praise God and thank Him for all He is and has done. It is shameful to pray only when you want something.

A special type of praying is "shared prayer" — when followers of Christ pray together. This is helpful to all, since we can learn from one another and can encourage one another in prayer.

Prayers before and after meals are appropriate and are recommended — aloud if in a Catholic or Christian setting, and privately if in a public setting.

Remember also that prayer can be — and usually is — work. There are times when it is very hard work. Be prepared for boredom, tedium, dissatisfaction. There are many times when you will not want to pray or when you seem to get nothing from it. Be able to bite the bullet and to go right on, since you are not doing it for personal satisfaction but rather in gratitude to God and in imitation of Jesus Christ.

As much as you can, avoid rushing through prayers. Do not be mechanical or thoughtless. This is a constant challenge when you have set prayers to say, such as the Breviary or the rosary. Aim for quality above quantity, and so control your life and mind so that you manage time and are not rushed when praying.

There are many other ideas about prayer that could be mentioned. These, however, are given in the hope that they will help you pray, now in this modern age, as a mature follower of the Lord Jesus should be praying.

How Should A Catholic
Live the Faith?

Some basic questions have been faced already: why you ought to believe in God...accept Jesus Christ as your Lord and Savior...be a convinced member of the Catholic Church...and hold the teachings of the Catholic Church.

This last section is most important. How does a Catholic go about living the faith? This goes beyond just believing— this is living. You have to develop a "philosophy of life." Like a farmer growing a crop, you have to work at your faith. You have to cultivate your religious life.

In this modern and scientific age, how does a person lead a quality Catholic life? The job is different than it was a century ago, or even 10 years ago. To say "love God and keep the Commandments of God and of the Church" is not enough for the modern world.

The problem today is deeper. It is a problem of the spirit by which you live. How can you lead a quality religious life and at the same time buck the headwinds of modern living? The unending noise, the constant change, the latest styles, the thousands of smiling hucksters, money problems, crime, worry over the future, etc. In such an atmosphere, how can Christ and holiness and peace and the state of grace come through? When many are sick at heart and destroying themselves, how can you live out your days so as to keep the Christ in you strong?

You can get much help from the Gospels and from the ancient wisdom of the Catholic Church. Here are Ten Rules for Living—for living a balanced Catholic life in today's world.

Rule 1: learn to forget yourself

Unless in life you forget yourself, you will remain a prisoner in the narrowest of prisons. The Lord said: "If anyone wishes to be a follower of mine, he must leave self behind" (Luke 9:23). The job is somehow to die to self, and then to live for others. "I tell you a grain of wheat remains a solitary grain unless it falls into the ground and dies; but if it dies, it bears a rich harvest. The man who loves himself is lost..." (John 12:24-25).

The self-centered person goes through life looking at the end of his nose, always trying to impress others, subjected to needless worries and tensions, liable to be filled with the self-love which is pride. Self-forgetfulness is another name for humility—the basic quality of a good life. Try to avoid thinking and talking of yourself. Learn self-forgetfulness.

Rule 2: develop a prayer-union with God

To live a genuine spiritual life, you must pray—pray every day, and pray often. This is essential. How do you learn how to pray? A prayerful Catholic—a priest, religious or lay person—might be able to help you.

I suggest that you start by learning the value of silence. The unending noises of TV and radio can make life more interesting, but they can keep you from thinking your own thoughts, from possessing your own soul in peace, and from praying. You will need "quiet time" in your life every day.

Try to get a book of helpful prayers. Every morning read morning prayers. Before every single meal offer your thanks to God, either aloud or in your thoughts. Every day take ten to fifteen minutes in quiet to read the Bible or other spiritual book. When life permits, go to daily Mass or make a visit of prayer in church. Try to praise God in your prayers. End each day with night prayers.

Have some good religious art where you live. Develop your personal devotions, following the rhythms of the liturgy. Grow into a life of contemplation. Make a retreat when you can.

This is personal prayer—the kind mentioned in Matthew 6:6. (The public prayer of Sunday Mass is something different.) This is your personal daily prayer-union with God, and it is basic for spiritual living.

"Develop a 'philosophy of life.' Like a farmer growing a crop, you have to work at your faith. You have to cultivate your religious life."

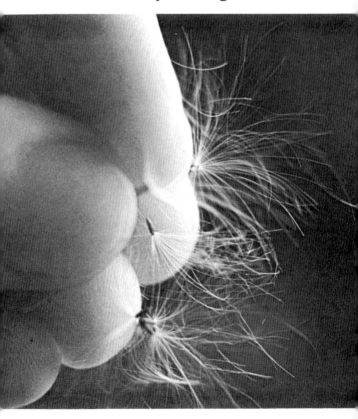

Rule 3: be interested in others and help all other people

Once a person has learned to forget self, then it is possible to accomplish something worthwhile in life. Then a person does not clutter up this earth like the selfish, barren fig tree. You should then be genuinely interested in others. And the Lord makes it clear that you are to be at peace with all men, interested in all children of God, trying to help as many of them as you can. To help others becomes then your way of life—and not a part-time hobby. In this you show yourself a follower of Christ.

Rule 4: never be critical of others

The spirit of the modern world is to judge others critically, to challenge their motives. But you are not to be negative or critical. Others may hold a person guilty until proven innocent; for you, all others are innocent until proven guilty. These rules for judgment of others are given in the Sermon on the Mount (cf. Matthew 7:1-5). The critic harms self more than the one criticized. An ancient Roman saying was: "Concerning the dead, say only good things." Your rule of life must be to say only good things about the living as well as the dead.

Rule 5: cultivate the spirit of joy

This rule is of great importance for those people who see only the bad of the present and only the good of the past. Within the framework of your life today, make your own happiness.

This is easy to do if you have the spirit of joy coming from the "good news" of the risen Christ. And it is easier to do if you have a saving sense of humor, plus a real interest in religious, cultural and intellectual questions. Within the frame of your life today are hundreds of helps to make your own happiness—even in the most humdrum location, and in times of constant crisis.

Rule 6: live in the living present

God in His wisdom has given us life divided into days and nights. The wise person learns to take life each day as it comes, to put into each day its quota of prayer, work and education — and then to get an earned night's sleep in preparation for the next day. "So do not be anxious about tomorrow; tomorrow will look after itself. Each day has troubles enough of its own" (Matthew 6:34). We should not think today of yesterday's mistakes or of tomorrow's worries. Live in the living present, "heart within and God o'erhead."

Rule 7: want no material thing

You are close to wisdom and happiness if and when you can say to yourself that there is really no material thing that you want or need. The Lord, Son of God, was born poor, lived as a poor man, and died owning nothing. Simplicity in living is a blessing — we moderns can so complicate living that we lose all peace of mind.

Rule 8: never divorce Christ from His Church

You must expect, as life goes along, to see weaknesses in the Church. Just as you are not perfect, so others in the Church (popes, bishops, priests, for example) have not always been perfect. You may be unhappy over some teaching, some sermon, some newspaper story. You may think that the Church or its representatives are not representing Christ.

At such times remember that Christ Himself started this Church building it on the imperfect Peter. That same Church is the bride of Christ (look at Ephesians 5:22-33) — and you cannot divorce them. Christ is the head of the body, the Church (look at Colossians 1:18) — and never try to cut off that Head. You are a Catholic because of Christ, and for no other reason.

Rule 9: build up your own parish

Your link with the universal Church is through your own parish. A parish is a geographical area. You live in a parish. Some Catholics of a certain national descent have a national parish.

Being a Catholic means strengthening your own parish, and encouraging and helping the priest who is your pastor. Whenever you move, register in your parish and do your level best to encourage the priests and the other parishioners.

It is easy to become a dropout from parish life—to avoid registering, to be a nonsupporter, to start going to Sunday Mass at other parishes, to go to Sunday Mass in a private chapel. But an important feature of Catholic life is strengthening your own parish—helping your own parish priests and your fellow parishioners of all ages.

Rule 10: lead a sacramental life

You must sort out values in life and put first things first. In gratitude to God you observe the first day of each week as the Lord's Day. Sunday Mass is at the top of the week's schedule. And at every Mass you should receive Holy Communion, the nourishment of your soul. With the help of regular confession, stay and grow in the state of God's grace. Learn the customs and rules for politeness in Church, so that you will do what is right and proper in Church, and feel at home in God's house.

Conclusion

This Catholic faith is a jewel—our most valuable possession. Like a jewel it has many sides, many facets—Christ Jesus, Head of the Church...St. Peter, the Rock foundation... certainty in doctrine...the Holy Father...the Mass...the help of the sacraments...the call to holiness...personal devotions. And of this remarkable value we are the poorest salesmen, the weakest advertisers. We have been given so much by God— and should do much more in appreciation.

Daughters of St. Paul

MASSACHUSETTS
  50 St. Paul's Ave., Jamaica Plain, Boston, MA 02130 **617-522-8911.**
  172 Tremont Street, Boston, MA 02111 **617-426-5464; 617-426-4230.**

NEW YORK
  78 Fort Place, Staten Island, NY 10301 **718-447-5071; 718-447-5086.**
  59 East 43rd Street, New York, NY 10017 **212-986-7580.**
  625 East 187th Street, Bronx, NY 10458 **212-584-0440.**
  525 Main Street, Buffalo, NY 14203 **716-847-6044.**

NEW JERSEY
  Hudson Mall Route 440 and Communipaw Ave.,
    Jersey City, NJ 07304 **201-433-7740.**

CONNECTICUT
  202 Fairfield Ave., Bridgeport, CT 06604 **203-335-9913.**

OHIO
  2105 Ontario Street (at Prospect Ave.), Cleveland, OH 44115 **216-621-9427.**
  616 Walnut Street, Cincinnati, OH 45202 **513-421-5733; 513-721-5059.**

PENNSYLVANIA
  1719 Chestnut Street, Philadelphia, PA 19103 **215-568-2638; 215-864-0991.**

VIRGINIA
  1025 King Street, Alexandria, VA 22314 **703-549-3806.**

SOUTH CAROLINA
  243 King Street, Charleston, SC 29401 **803-577-0175.**

FLORIDA
  2700 Biscayne Blvd., Miami, FL 33137 **305-573-1618.**

LOUISIANA
  4403 Veterans Memorial Blvd. Metairie, LA 70006 **504-887-7631; 504-887-0113.**
  423 Main Street, Baton Rouge, LA 70802 **504-343-4057; 504-381-9485.**

MISSOURI
  1001 Pine Street (at North 10th), St. Louis, MO 63101 **314-621-0346.**

ILLINOIS
  172 North Michigan Ave., Chicago, IL 60601 **312-346-4228; 312-346-3240.**

TEXAS
  114 Main Plaza, San Antonio, TX 78205 **512-224-8101.**

CALIFORNIA
  1570 Fifth Ave. (at Cedar Street), San Diego, CA 92101 **619-232-1442.**
  46 Geary Street, San Francisco, CA 94108 **415-781-5180.**

WASHINGTON
  2301 Second Ave., Seattle, WA 98121 **206-441-3300.**

HAWAII
  1143 Bishop Street, Honolulu, HI 96813 **808-521-2731.**

ALASKA
  750 West 5th Ave., Anchorage, AK 99501 **907-272-8183.**

CANADA
  3022 Dufferin Street, Toronto 395, Ontario, Canada.